Autism's Hidden Blessings

Discovering God's Promises
for Autistic Children & Their Families

Kelly Langston

Kregel
Publications

Autism's Hidden Blessings: Discovering God's Promises for Autistic Children and Their Families

© 2009 by Kelly Langston

Published by Kregel Publications, a division of Kregel, Inc., P.O. Box 2607, Grand Rapids, MI 49501.

The author and publisher are not engaged in rendering medical or psychological services, and this book is not intended as a guide to diagnose or treat medical or psychological problems. If medical, psychological, or other expert assistance is required by the reader, please seek the services of your own physician or certified counselor.

Cover photograph of Alec Langston by Charles N. Jenkins, July 2006. Used by permission. Other photographs taken June 2008.

Library of Congress Cataloging-in-Publication Data
Langston, Kelly
    Autism's hidden blessings : discovering God's promises for autistic children and their families / Kelly Langston.
        p. cm.
    Includes bibliographical references.
    1. Parents of autistic children—Religious life. 2. Parents of children with disabilities—Religious life. 3. Autism in children. I. Title.
    BV4596.P35L36 2009 248.8'619685882—dc22 2008056108

ISBN 978-0-8254-2977-4

Printed in the United States of America

09 10 11 12 13 / 5 4 3 2 1

Autism's
Hidden
Blessings

To all of God's unique, blessed, and beautiful children
who walk this earth with a special need.

Your very presence here teaches us more than any book ever
could. Know this: God's heart—which has no limit—is for you!
You are greatly valued and loved beyond your wildest dreams.

Oh, that I might comfort some of my Master's servants. I have written out of my own heart with the view of comforting their hearts. I would say to them in their trials—My brethren, God is good. He will not forsake you: He will bear you through.

CHARLES HADDON SPURGEON

Contents

Preface

Throughout the writing of this book I've had you in mind. You're the parent or loved one of a child with autism. I'm so thankful for the opportunity to walk this journey with you, if only for the time it takes you to read this book. We are, after all, walking in similar shoes. I have no doubt that God led you to pick up this book. He has been leading me, in fact, to write it for a number of years as He walked with our family through times of darkness.

I remember the day when Alec was first diagnosed, when we received from the team of specialists evaluating our son the unexpected words, "Your son suffers from an autism spectrum disorder."[1] They each offered us a formal handshake, the last pressing a thin brochure into my hand as they ushered us out the door. We knew nothing about autism then and had no idea what to do next as we slumped out into the fog of that morning. We were speechless, like our son, knowing our entire lives had changed. Looking back on those days, I see now that God not only walked with us, but carried us as well.

There have been days when I've sat on a curb in tears. I'd tried to get Alec into his school building for a preschool party, a pizza in one hand and my son in the car, refusing to get out, kicking and screaming in a tantrum that could shatter glass. Other times I've rolled over and over on the carpet with him, wrestling shoes onto his chubby feet. This was during January, but despite the cold, he couldn't stand to wear them. I've sat on the side of Alec's bed at night and cried out to God, *Oh Lord! I want Alec to know You! How can I teach him about You when he can't even speak with me?*

We've also had moments of fantastic victory, like watching Alec in the kindergarten school play, singing every word to every song; or seeing him argue with his older sister, Elise, just like any little brother would do. I've treasured the sight of him jumping off the afternoon school bus with his arms wide, rushing into my arms, and I've thought, *Lord, what a blessing to receive such love!*

Dear reader, I don't know where you are on this journey. But wherever it is, I want you to know that God has a message for you and your child with autism.

That message is this:

> Your child is greatly loved by God.
> Your child is greatly valued by God.
> God has a wonderful purpose for your child's life,
> No less than that of any other child.

And here's something else: God never intended for you, as a parent, to walk this journey alone! In fact, He has given you powerful treasures in His Scripture that will give you wings to soar above the oppressive grip of autism. No matter how overwhelmed you might feel, no matter what challenges you face, financial burdens, stress, weariness, or even intense loneliness, know this: God gave you this child for a reason. God believes in you, and He is for you!

This is why I'm writing this book. I want you to know that you are not alone, and never have been. No matter whether you are a single parent, or a married couple, or a loved one trying to support a family dealing with autism, God has a message for you and the child you love. And He has provided mighty tools to overcome autism.

While this book does offer helpful resources for parents and loved ones of autistic children, it is not intended as a medical manual for dealing with autism. Rather, this book encourages you to discover the promises that God has made, to claim those promises, and to apply them to your life and the life of your child living with autism.

Never doubt for a minute that God loves your child with a love so wide and long and high and deep that we cannot comprehend its measure. God, who has woven every cell and every DNA strand together, knew your baby before you ever laid a kiss to his cheek, and He has chosen *you* to parent him for a specific reason. He sees your potential to nurture this special being that He has placed in your arms to help him become all that He intended him to be.

Did you know that God has a treasure box of promises stored up in His Word for us and our little ones? These promises can strengthen us and can provide hope, wisdom, and direction on how to care for our uniquely made, incredibly beautiful kids—kids created by God's own hand to serve an extraordinary purpose!

Did you know that, through Christ, God gives us everything—and I mean everything—we need to carry us through in this battle with autism? And we will more than survive the battle; we will conquer autism with an overflowing and abundant joy in our lives such as we have never known!

If you will seek to really know God, even as you are doing in reading this book, and if you study and apply the precious promises of God to your family life, then the sun will shine again on your walk and you will feel its warmth return to your days. You will break forth into singing, with a new song, one of strength and confidence in place of worry, fear, and stress. God's truth is this: We have nothing to fear. He is for our children.

The book in your hands presumes that you have a working knowledge of autism. If, however, you're unfamiliar with autism spectrum disorders (ASDs), I have placed two sources of information at the end of this book to help you learn more. In Appendix A—"What Is Autism?"—you'll find helpful information including statistical data and a list of signs and symptoms of the disorder for early diagnosis and intervention. Appendix B—"Autism Resources"—lists books and online resources for therapies and treatments, as well as places to go for support and further information.

Are you ready? Come on, then! Let's take a journey into the scriptural promises of God. Let's uncover them, one by one, holding them up to the light, turning them over in our minds. Let's try them out. The Bible says "Taste and see that the LORD is good. How happy is the man who takes refuge in Him!" (Ps. 34:8).

My personal promise to you is this: God's promises will profoundly change the way you think about autism. As you study them, I pray that God will lift the veil from your eyes so you can see your child as God does: entirely beautiful, full of value and worth, precious in every way, and filled to the brim with a powerful, special purpose.

These promises will make a vast difference in your life. You will smile again. You will laugh again. You will love more than you ever thought possible, and as you open your heart fully, allowing God to love your child through you, your arms will be His arms; your smile, His smile. You'll be filled with the majesty of a love that knows no limit and no end. It's a miraculous love that only strengthens and multiplies when poured out. It cannot be contained.

In this process you'll receive an added blessing; you'll get a glimpse of the magnitude of God's love for *you*. You'll understand a little more about the wondrous mystery of love itself. And you'll be empowered to pass on God's wisdom to others on this journey.

Yes, I've had you in mind. So let's get started, shall we?

Blessed are you who are hungry now,
because you will be filled.
Blessed are you who weep now,
because you will laugh.
Luke 6:21

Acknowledgments

It takes a village to raise a child. The truth in this old adage, commonly attributed to an African proverb and popularized by Hillary Rodham Clinton, is never more obvious than when the child in question is autistic. To list all of the many people who have helped our family is not possible. Each day our family receives a new gift of kindness from someone, and in each of these persons we are forever blessed.

That said, I thank all of Alec's teachers and caregivers who have welcomed my son into their arms. Where would we be without teachers who see only the possibility—not the disability—of a child: teachers like Sue Ann Belcher, Crystal Lail, Deborah Mullen, Natalie Whitaker, and Amanda Eisel? We watched our son literally reconnect to this world through the caring hands of Julie Thompson, Betsy Spaeth, Wyndi Stitt, Sharae Lattimore, Tammy Cone, Nancy Dill, Carol George, Susan Fletcher, and Michelle Goode. And how many times have I thanked God for the courage and prayers of Susan Kincaid, Karen Apple, Robin Gladden, Betty Bogart, and Beth Berkland?

I could never forget school principals like Rachel McKenzie and Martha Carpenter who provide welcoming school environments to every child, regardless of disability. May God bless you in abundance for each provision of love you give to autistic children in your schools. They are worth your efforts.

I can't tell you how heartening it has been to have Candace Wilson of the Council for Children's Rights stand with our family. In fact, God bless all the advocates out there!

Many children have been real-life heroes in Alec's life, such as

George and Sam Hunter, Jerrod Gervasi, Cassidy Calbreath, Lily Farr, Keegan Ruark, Andrew Utesch, Ryan Pierce, Bradley Thompson, Grantley Bone, Hee Lim Kim, Christopher Pendleton, Joshua Lee, and Ben Stokely. You looked beyond autism and welcomed my son as a good friend. What an example you are! You have no idea what you have meant to our family.

Whenever the darkness of autism closed in, I always could call on other autism moms to share some of their wisdom. Quite simply, autism never stood a chance against the remarkable strength of women like Colleen Jenny, Beth Fields, Melissa Myers, Pam McCarthy, Tracy Reed, Betsy Spaeth, Deanne Nelson, Sally Miller, and Jill Urwick. Ladies, Jeremiah 31:16–17 is for you!

Jennifer Krueger, do you see how powerful one word of encouragement can be? And to my prayer warriors—Nan Henderson, June Davies, Joy Stuart, and Debbie and Dean Gutch—and our Bible study group, thank you for every single prayer. God heard each one.

I can't forget the people at Kregel Publications, who made writing this book a joy.

And of course, I must thank my family members and friends who are with us in the battle. To Mary Ann and Norman Langston and Margaret and Dan Saltrick—thanks for listening, caring, and being there. Your smiles have lightened our load. To my sisters and brothers-in-law Wendy and Michael Jones, Rachel and Tim Taylor, and Sarah Richards—thanks for allowing me to be me, even when I wasn't so fun to be around, and for providing laughter when we desperately needed it. A special thanks to my sister Amanda Hankins, who selflessly offered many prayers and words of comfort—you are one of the greatest blessings in my life.

To my mother, Susan Grimm, who shaped my life as she dried the tears from my cheeks when I was young—from you, Mom, I learned what love can do, and I will never forget it. I love you so much!

To my father, Ted Smith, who was crazy enough to believe me when I told him I felt God's call to write this book. Your faith is amazing! Thanks for the countless calls during the process of writing it. Dad, you have been my sounding board, and this book would not exist without your input, advice, prayers, and support. So many times you kept me going. I love you, Dad, and I trust that all four coin cans are finally mine. You know what I mean.

Thanks to you, Elise, my sweet daughter. You are Alec's best teacher and have melted my heart with your compassion and sweet spirit. What plans God must have for you! I gaze at you in awe, knowing God is painting your life with the most beautiful of colors. Never be afraid to speak out for people who need a voice. God is with you, my child.

To my sweet Matt, who sacrificed daily with me to write and live out this book: you are my hero. I have no idea why God blessed me with a man like you, but I thank Him every single day for doing it. You never complained, never gave up, and always believed in the impossible. Matt, you have the entirety of my heart . . . and you always will.

And certainly not in the least, thank you, Alec, for teaching me the power of love. Your story is only beginning, my son, and I will forever be cheering you on. God moved mountains to rescue you! Thank you for the joy that I have found in being your mom. Now I am the speechless one.

But above all, this book would not be in your hands if it were not for my Father and His precious son, Jesus. As I wrote it, I could feel an overwhelming magnitude of love for children with autism and their families. There is nothing more powerful than God's love. It moves mountains and heals broken hearts, and has changed me forever. This is His story.

Life's Detour

Landing on the Dark Road of Autism

*Now we see but a poor reflection as in a mirror; then we shall
see face to face. Now I know in part; then I shall know fully,
even as I am fully known.*

1 Corinthians 13:12 (NIV)

I didn't know he was autistic.

I didn't, in fact, know anything about autism. As it did for so many
people, the movie *Rainman* provided the only description of autism I
knew at the time.

I did know, however, that a "good mother"—an adept mother—
should discipline an unruly toddler into compliance before the child
gets too big to handle. I'd heard this parenting rule many times. A
greenhorn of mothering with only a few years of experience under my
belt, I was on a constant hunt for golden nuggets of advice from the
parenting experts of the day, militantly studying their recommendations like I once studied my collegiate courses.

I also knew everything about the bathroom at Target. It is cold,
with five bright red stalls, four porcelain sinks, and glossy white walls
that echoed the swats I rendered to my son's behind to obtain the compliance that every good mother requires. I sought refuge in this room
whenever Alec threw a tantrum in the store, which was about every
time we visited Target during his toddler years.

Our local Target was a place to go to grab a cold soda from the snack
bar and get out of the energy-sapping, North Carolina sun. Saturated

with sweat and boredom, I took Alec and Elise there when I needed a break from their toddler world, if only in terms of surroundings. I went to Target to hear an adult voice in days filled with Playhouse Disney shows, nursery rhymes, and little toy trains. The store is large and always full of mothers toting along their smart-looking children. They were families that looked as if they came right off of the pages of *Family Circle* magazine.

In my frequent retreats to the bathroom to wait out one of Alec's fits, I'd smile apologetically to the mothers as they entered the room. I'd try to act like I had Alec under my control.

I didn't, of course.

Looking back, I don't recall exactly when Alec transitioned from an engaging infant to a challenging child. But once Alec reached his toddler years, I frequently found myself in stormy situations that took every ounce of my strength and limited parenting wisdom to navigate.

Typical family gatherings and holidays were becoming a source of stress for our family. Even Halloween. I thought every child loved to don a costume and canvass the neighborhood for treats. My older daughter bubbled with pure joy as she toddled around in her cow outfit, proudly smiling at the "awwwws" of neighbors as they tossed candy into her small plastic pumpkin. Yet two years later, Alec sat on our living room floor in that same cow outfit, his face purple and twisted in rage. He tugged and pulled at the fake fur, making every effort to discard it. Eventually, I left him at home with my husband, Matt, and took Big Sister Elise, in disguise as Eeyore, to enjoy the night collecting candy.

On our way to play in the park that same winter, I rehearsed my canned explanations. Other mothers at the park would point out that it was, in fact, quite cold outside and my son wasn't wearing his shoes. *Yes, I know*, I'd think bitterly. A little bit of cold weather couldn't convince my two-year-old to leave his shoes on his plump little feet in the park.

It seemed strange to me that Alec demanded events to be in a specific order. With no knowledge of the obsessive-compulsive tendencies often found in children with autism, I couldn't understand why Alec was such a "difficult" child. Over time, as if by unintentional conditioning, I discovered that life was less problematic when I did things in the order and manner that Alec preferred. This was easier said than done because Alec couldn't communicate with words. His pediatrician assured me Alec was merely a late bloomer in terms of speech. So I was forced to play guessing games to determine what Alec wanted at any given moment, and it was a source of increasing frustration for both of us. Out of the blue, Alec's ripple of fussiness would become a tsunami of violence and power.

One afternoon I wasn't adhering to my son's unspoken plan during our shopping trip. Once again I'd managed to hit the invisible trip wire activating Alec's ear-shattering screams. So commenced The Guessing Game.

"What do you want, Alec?" I anxiously asked, well aware of the glances from the *Family Circle* moms around me. Alec responded by screaming louder, pressing his chubby palms to his ears.

No stranger to this game, I frantically searched everything around me trying to locate the source of Alec's distress. "Alec, do you want this book?" I asked, grabbing the nearest item and hoping to distract him. To this suggestion, my brawny son began kicking me from his seat in the cart, his shrieks an earsplitting 11 on a scale of 1 to 10.

In tantrum mode, Alec was a pint-sized Tasmanian Devil transformed from cartoon to flesh. People peered down the aisle at the unpleasant scene and scurried away. An elderly woman rolled her eyes and glared at me. Parents grabbed their children by the hand and vacated the area. As I struggled with my son, I felt the sting of everyone's unspoken question: *Can't you control your child?*

Here we go again, God. Now what do I do? The tantrum intensified despite my efforts to soothe my frustrated son. Nothing seemed to work, and tears of embarrassment over my own incompetence slid down my cheeks. I looked at my shopping cart of items I needed at home and considered how to wrestle my son out of it and bolt out of the store.

God, what am I doing wrong?

I'm convinced that God leaned down and sent help my way. My

mother-in-law, Mary Ann Langston—a well-educated woman with a Midas touch in social situations— unexpectedly appeared by my side. She seemed to have been teleported from some other world to this aisle of our ongoing battle.

"I was on the other side of the store," she explained gingerly, with an unsure expression on her face, "and I recognized that cry."

She could hear it all the way across the store? Still, I was never so glad to see someone in my life! She swiftly pulled Alec from his seat, took my shopping cart, and ushered us to the exit so I could take my distraught son home while she stayed behind to pay for all my items. Blood seeped from my bitten lip as I fought back tears and walked Alec outside, ending yet another battle at Target.

As the year went on I learned small tricks to deal with Alec's tantrums. One was The Preschool Shuffle. I learned the locations of the exits at my son's morning preschool. I'd discovered that if I picked up Alec just five minutes late from our church preschool, I could miss the other mothers retrieving their children. This small delay would spare those mothers from the daily episode of Alec angrily beating my back as I carried him tossed over my shoulder—the only way I could transition him out of the classroom—down the hallways to the nearest and most isolated exit.

At the time, I didn't know if Alec was just a demanding child, or if I simply bore the humiliation of being an inept mother. With each passing day I was filled with more pain as my son's frustrations increased. A mother wants only to comfort her children when they're in despair. Alec was struggling but I had no idea how to help him. With every beat of my mother's heart, I wanted to believe that, in spite of Alec's daily fits of rage, deep inside he was a sweet little boy desperate to be understood—and I wanted others to know him in this same way. But how could I reach him?

I needed more advice!

Once more, I scoured the Internet, news columns, and books for recommendations from the parenting gurus who worked with difficult children. The predominant advice was to provide stringent consequences for unacceptable behavior. The *Charlotte Observer*, for example, runs a weekly column from a nationally respected expert in parenting. Matt and I read his column every week and usually agreed with his advice. An authority in helping parents bring strong-willed children to obedience, he encourages parents to grow a backbone and stop allowing their children to run the family. He advises parents to incorporate strong and persuasive consequences for bad behavior.

This must be what our Alec needs. I thought. *Alec is simply a strong-willed child.*

Determined to succeed, Matt and I began a zero-tolerance policy for bad behavior. Alec would get one warning to get in line with our expectations and if not, we began consequences. Typically, this meant a time out or an exile to his room. If the behavior persisted, we would in no way back down. If Alec acted out physically by hitting or kicking, he would receive a swat to the behind.

Matt and I formed a cohesive parenting front against Alec's numerous daily tantrums. We were certain that by uniting as strong parents, we could stop the tantrums.

What we didn't understand, though, was that Alec was not a strong-willed child. Unbeknown to us he was suffering from *sensory integration dysfunction.* This condition is experienced by many children on the autism spectrum. Their developing brains are not able to correctly process the barrage of information pouring into their senses. Bright lights, for instance, stabbed at Alec's steel blue eyes. Ordinary noises clashed like cymbals in his ears. Further, he was hyposensitive to touch, which meant he would constantly smack and crash into things, or people, in order to receive sufficient stimulation to find himself spatially.

My Alec was living in a bizarre world that his tiny body was not able to translate for him. My son was in pain. He was calling out for help, but I didn't understand him. He was a child without the ability to communicate his needs to his own mother. I'm not proud of the fact that I was totally oblivious to what was really going on with my son. Instead of seeing Alec's critical need, we continued on with our tough-love policy.

Winning the Battle, Losing the War

One of the biggest battles in this war for compliance was The Battle of the Chicken Bite.

A typical problem many kids on the autism spectrum share is that they don't want to sit down for meals. And many are self-limiting in terms of what they eat due to sensory issues—foods that taste good to us are overwhelming in flavor or texture to them. Suddenly you're faced with a child who won't eat.

My son's bill of fare was limited to a small handful of foods: peanut butter crackers, pizza, french fries, bacon, pretzels, and occasionally some starchy cereal. Let's see, what am I forgetting? Hmmmm. Nothing, I guess. No fruit . . . unless you count Fruit Roll-ups. I don't think so. No veggies . . . unless you count the potato in the french fries, which is a starch. But I was desperate enough to consider it a vegetable.

No doubt, a good mother wouldn't let her child eat such an unhealthy and limited diet. Determined to be a good mom to this boy, I was going to set him straight and get him to eat!

On a sunny September day, I prepared for the battle to get Alec to try some chicken. He was scrounging for pretzels and junk food at the time, so I quickly nuked the chicken with some french fries and sat Alec down. Then I ordered him to stay in his chair until he tried one bite of the bland white meat.

Alec started to get up. Determined to grow a backbone, I said, "Alec, if you take one bite, you can get up and play. Just one bite."

This was an easy offer, after all. *Maybe too easy*, I thought. Alec tried to slide off his chair so I put my hand on the seat to trap him there. I did not budge. He began to cry, so I pleaded with him, "Alec, if you take one bite, then you can get up."

The cries became sobs, then deafening wails, but I remained calm and resolute. It was a warm day and every window of our home was open to let in the fresh air. That also, of course, made all the neighbors privy to the table war going on inside our home.

Alec stood his ground with fierce screaming and wails. His little round fists beat the table. His stout legs kicked his chair and my arms. It sounded like I was torturing him, but I was only preventing him from sliding off of his seat. I'd never heard such earsplitting shrieks.

Five minutes passed . . . then ten. Then fifteen, and twenty, and the screaming escalated. I began to worry. *What are the neighbors going to think? The police will be showing up at my door any minute. Surely Children's Services will be notified to take my son into their custody!* Beads of sweat covered my forehead. *Should I cave in to him? What would the parenting experts say?*

Then forty-seven horrid minutes from the start of our battle, Alec put *one bite* of chicken into his mouth.

"Good, Alec!" I exclaimed with tears of joy running down my face. I was eager to pull my son into my arms and end this torturous battle. "Just chew it up and swallow it and you can get up to play!"

And my exhausted, sweaty son did just that. I had won this battle! I was a tough mother capable of bringing my strong-willed child into compliance! I had a backbone!

And then in that split-second moment of victory, Alec threw up.

God, what am I doing wrong? Why won't he just do what he needs to do? Our war for compliance continued. It seemed that every day was filled with sickening tantrums. Alec spent more and more daily episodes in his time-out chair. I feared going into public places, knowing that I'd probably have to leave, dragging my son back to the car in a violent fit. In the process, I became proficient at avoiding the eyes of other mothers in stores so I wouldn't have to explain my son's behavior.

Each day I got out of bed determined to mother my son with love, compassion, strength, and a backbone. But by the afternoon my determination had faded, my head hurt, and my heart ached as I tried to understand why my son did not respond to our disciplinary tactics. The worst part was that some intuition informed me that my son was not a little monster. When I looked into his eyes, I was sure I saw light in there. I sensed that deep inside he truly wanted to be a good son and make me smile, and I clung to the belief that he truly wanted to please me.

Now over two years old, Alec was still not able to communicate in words to me. He didn't even call me "Mama." He spoke mostly gibberish, but at times he would repeat an exact phrase from a cartoon. *Should this count as language?* I wondered. I took him to his pediatrician again to help determine if Alec's lack of language was a problem.

"Don't expect a boy to learn to communicate as quickly as your daughter," she instructed me. Matt and I had written down Elise's repertoire of expressions when she was eighteen months old. They added up to over sixty-five words. *True, Elise is exceptionally bright,* I tried to reason away my concerns. *I must be an overly concerned mother. I just need to relax and ease up on my expectations for Alec.*

But the fact that I could count on one hand Alec's two-year-old vocabulary remained unsettling. I longed to converse with my son. How could I teach and instruct my son without words?

Months went by as Matt and I struggled to grow our backbones. We were discouraged to find that our zero-tolerance policy was not resulting in the more stable, happier child the parenting experts had promised. Instead, I was now a frazzled, self-doubting mother on the verge of a nervous breakdown. Even worse, my beautiful son, Alec, was an emotional mess showing no signs of improvement.

Looking back, I realize that up to this point I hadn't truly sought the wisdom of God. My silent appeals to God had been merely pleas, not real prayers—not a decision to turn our struggle over to God. I don't know why Matt and I didn't run to God for help with Alec in the first place. He is the Creator. He made every neuron, every combination of DNA, and every cell. God's Word confirms this: "Before I formed you in the womb I knew you" (Jer. 1:5 NIV). Why did I spend so much time seeking help from experts who had never met my son, when the One who masterfully knit my son within me had all of the answers?

I didn't know it yet, but I had an extraordinary Helper who was just waiting for me to surrender my battle and call His name. God promises to grant us wisdom in any situation if only we ask Him. "If any of you lacks wisdom, he should ask God, who gives generously to all without finding fault, and it will be given to him" (James 1:5 NIV). I'd searched every other resource, however, before I cried out to the Father for help.

When I at last raised the white flag and called, God, who never forsakes us, came and removed the veil from my eyes. Before I had merely hoped that I'd sensed a spark of willingness in Alec. God now granted me one moment, both marvelous and terrible, when I looked into Alec's face and clearly saw the anguish in my son's soul.

Through a Glass, Darkly

The day I called out to God and was answered was particularly taxing, filled with nasty battles with Alec. He had fought my every request, kicking, screaming at me, and refusing to comply with anything I asked. Nothing was going right that day.

I could feel my blood pressure rising and my face heating. As he lay prostrate on the floor, screaming, my ears were aching, my back was sore from wrestling his clothes on, and my internal pitcher of love was quite empty. I was about to lose control.

This was a moment when I should have walked away. I should have called for help. I should have disappeared upstairs, taken a few deep breaths, counted to twenty, or anything other than what I did. I should have known.

But I didn't.

It was a moment I'd give anything to live over. Have you ever had one of those? It's a memory that cuts so deeply into my soul that it may never heal. It left a scar so dark, it may never completely fade. It was a moment of brutal honesty when God pulled away everything that kept me from seeing what is really inside of me, and it was terrifying.

All at once, a year's worth of rage and desperation exploded from my soul. I grabbed my son and plunged him onto the sofa. I then stood before him and screamed like I've never screamed before. In the face of my two-and-a-half-year-old son, I emptied my heart of its desperation. My face twisted with resentment, my eyes clenched shut, and my heart was devoid of understanding.

"Why can't you behave!?" I shouted at him. "Why can't you be good!?" On and on I railed at my little son.

And then I looked at him.

What I'd only sensed before was now plainly expressed in his body language. He was still sitting cross-legged on the sofa, but as I watched he seemed to collapse into himself. His little hands were clenched and his arms crossed over his chest as if in a fetal position. His little face was pinched in pain and tears, his mouth opened wide in silent sobs.

In incredible agony, I watched as he slouched forward, sinking even more into himself. Then my beautiful son turned away from me, like a little flower that felt unworthy of the sun's love.

My heart shattered in that very moment. In that instant, God removed the veil from my eyes, and I saw Alec's desperate desire to please me. I saw the torture he endured of not being understood, of not knowing how to communicate or how to love and be loved. I saw the grief, the pain, and, worst of all, the absence of hope.

And I understood. Alec was doing all that he could! He was trying to reach out to me, but he didn't know how. He was a prisoner, trapped in a troubled world that neither of us understood. The parenting experts were wrong. This child did not need stronger discipline. He needed more love. He needed me to go into that shadowy world and rescue him, to carry him out of that isolated place and back to us with the full authority of Christ's love.

In that terrible moment, I knew I had failed my son miserably.

My knees gave way and I sank to the floor, weeping. "God, oh, God! I need You so much! I see now. Help me be the mother that this child needs!"

Then God showed me what I had to do. I got up and scooped my weeping boy into my arms and carried him into the bathroom. I took a washcloth and dried his tears. I knelt before him and tenderly grasped his wet chin in my palm, lifting his face to my own.

"I'm coming to get you, Alec," I whispered and took him into my arms, holding on to him with every ounce of my being for what seemed like an eternity. "God will help me. I'm coming to get you, Alec."

And from that moment on, we were on a different road. There, God walked with us to guide the way, His love illuminating the darkness. God was leading our family back from the abyss and on to a new level of joy such as I had never experienced in all my life.

Yes, joy was to return, and it would bring along all of its companions: laughter, smiles, victories, promises, and most of all—hope.

Chapter 1

God's Promises
Our Lifeline to Overcome Autism

*You're blessed when you've lost it all. God's kingdom is there
for the finding. You're blessed when you're ravenously hungry.
Then you're ready for the Messianic meal. You're blessed
when the tears flow freely. Joy comes with the morning.*
Luke 6:20–21 (msg)

Joy? Blessed? I can hardly imagine what you might be thinking as you
read these verses from Luke. How can anyone be blessed in the face of
something as devastating as autism? In fact, you may blame God for
the hardship that autism has caused your family. At one time, I did,
too.

Where can you go when faced with the mountain of responsibilities involved in caring for a child with autism? What can you do when
hope seems so distant? Who will be there in the dead of the night
when you're alone with your sleepless child—children with autism often have sleep disorders. Where do you find light when you're afraid of
a future that seems so dark?

Who answers when you ask, "What will happen to my child? Am I
spiritually, physically, and mentally up to the demands of caring for a
child with special needs? What can I expect now that my life is drasti-
cally different than what I expected it to be?"

I know these questions well, because I've asked them, too. I've shared
your experiences. You've felt blood on your lips as you bite back the
tears, holding your precious child's hand as dreams of what could have

been fade away. You don't want to get out of bed in the morning, waking to an avalanche of responsibilities that overpower your thoughts before your feet even hit the floor. As you survey your current situation, taking everything in at once—every need, every concern, and every fear—how can you not feel overwhelmed?

Yes . . . I know the feeling. It's an emotion I fight daily myself. And yet I write to tell you that there is hope. And yes . . . I write to offer you some practical resources to help you in the fight. But I write mostly to tell you this: God does care about children with autism spectrum disorders (ASDs). Moreover, He has a special plan not only for your child, despite autism, but He has one for you, too! And He has given you promises that you can claim for you and your autistic child, and that you can live out daily.

If that's hard to believe, read on.

Life's Detour: A Turn onto the Dark Road of Autism

In early 2003, my husband, Matt, and I sat anxiously at a small conference table in a colorless room. Around the table sat a group of specialists who had just completed a series of tests on our then two-and-a-half-year-old son, Alec. After reviewing the results of each test, they uttered a word we never dreamed we'd hear in connection with our family: *autism*. At the pronouncement of that word, a fog descended upon us, threatening to suck away the room's oxygen.

The evaluation complete, we stood and thanked the specialists, offering weak smiles and handshakes all around, yet secretly despising them for every word they'd just said about our Alec. One of them pressed a small, repulsive beige pamphlet into our hands as we walked, bewildered, out the door.

Thinking back on that pamphlet, I recall only that unspeakable word *autism* on its cover. My *Rainman*-based definition of that word did not harmonize with my mind's vision of Alec's future—a strapping, gifted, and capable son running for touchdowns, scoring soccer goals, and surpassing all others on achievement tests.

It was a diagnosis I did not want for my son, Alec.

I looked at my husband after we walked back into the morning sunshine. We stared at each other, searching for words of comfort, but we had only silence to give. Everything around us buzzed by in warp speed while we struggled to make each step back to our van, our legs like lead, dragging a truth we had never considered. Everything was entirely different now, and we were not prepared for it. We felt so alone, as if the world had left us behind.

But we were never really alone.

Our family life had just turned onto a detour, a bizarre new road that we never knew existed. We had yet to realize that we'd begun an adventure that would color our lives in ways we could not imagine. Alec's autism would change us, but only for the better. Hard to believe? Yes, I know, but it's true.

A Light in the Darkness

Imagine this little drama for a moment. Trust me, it won't be hard.

A young couple have a beautiful toddler, a son who was once full of smiles and life, but now is slipping away from them. His vocabulary disappears and his smile is missing. He stops meeting the gaze of his parents. He's sick all of the time. He won't turn to Mom or Dad when they call his name.

So they have him tested. And the diagnosis? "It's autism."

The couple hires a slew of therapists. Speech therapists. Applied behavioral therapists. Occupational therapists. The couple consults with doctors and neurologists, and start to see progress.

Then the bills start rolling in. The insurance provider doesn't cover autism. Still, the child is improving, so the parents get a second mortgage and research area schools that specialize in helping children with autism spectrum disorders.

The months pass by and the bills pile up. Their nest egg dwindles away until nothing is left. Creditors begin calling, so Dad picks up some extra hours at work. Mom clips coupons and shops at discount stores and yard sales. The calls for payment on past due accounts are coming daily now. The economy takes a turn for the worse, bringing high gas prices and inflated food and clothing costs. Then the couples' old car blows its transmission again. More bills arrive, and they pay what they can but it's not enough. They hit rock bottom when Dad's position is outsourced overseas.

They are despondent!

Then one day the parents get a call from an attorney who wants the couple to come to his office immediately. Their hearts pound as they wonder what bombshell will drop next. The attorney sits down and looks at them.

"It seems my client," he begins, "a vastly notable gentleman, happens to be a patriarch of yours and has included you in his will."

"That can't be!" the mom exclaims. "We don't know of any patriarch who would leave us a dime!"

"Oh, yes," the attorney continues, "I have it all listed here. Many items of incredible value have been given to you."

"I don't believe it," the young dad is skeptical.

"Well," the attorney says, "you can believe it. It's all here in writing. I have the list here. All you have to do is accept them."

The attorney pulls out a contract with the couple's name written across the top with the word *beneficiary* beside it.

"This is you, correct?"

"Yes," says the young mom, "That's us."

As the attorney reads the items of their inheritance, page by page, gift by gift, a strange peace falls over the couple as they realize that their benefactor has bequeathed resources that will answer their every need. Nothing is left for them to do but accept the gifts and put them to good use.

Does this sound like an implausible story?

You do, indeed, have a benefactor who loves you so much that he has left you a treasure of great worth. That benefactor is God, the great I AM, and those treasures are His promises for His children. They are written in Scripture—His sacred Word, penned throughout the course of history and divinely inspired by Him—and they are signed by Christ. For every need you will ever have, God has graciously given a promise. These promises can strengthen us and can provide hope, wisdom, and direction for how to care for our uniquely made, incredibly beautiful kids.

Applying God's Promises to Your Life

Charles Haddon Spurgeon, the Billy Graham of his time, wrote *Faith's Checkbook*, a compilation of daily ponderings about the promises of God. In the preface he writes, "God has given no pledge which He will not redeem, and encouraged no hope which He will not fulfill."[1] Spurgeon provides an eye-opening comparison that relates a divine promise to a check made payable to believers:

> A promise from God may very instructively be compared to a check payable to order. It is given to the believer with the view of bestowing upon him some good thing. It is not meant that he should read it over comfortably, and then have done with it. No, he is to treat the promise as a reality, as a man treats a check.[2]

God never meant for us to wallow in the muck and mire of life's difficulties. He stocked His precious Word with promises to help us soar like eagles, to run and not grow weary through life's difficult circumstances. Yes, God intends for us to soar above autism. Why? So others will see His glory in us and be led to Him, and because He loves us and wants to be our God.

A check is merely worthless paper, unless it is cashed. And many Christians fail to draw on the treasury of God's promises to help them live the abundant life that Jesus desires for us. How, then, do we claim a promise and see it work in our lives? Again, Spurgeon answers this question in the allegory of the divine check:

> [A Christian] is to take the promise, and endorse it with his own name by personally receiving it as true. He is by faith to accept it as his own. He sets to his seal that God is true, and true as to this particular word of promise. He goes further, and believes that he has the blessing in having the sure promise of it and therefore he puts his name to it to testify to the receipt of the blessing.
>
> This done, he must believingly present the promise to the

Lord, as a man presents a check at the counter of the Bank. He must plead it by prayer, expecting to have it fulfilled. If he has come to Heaven's bank at the right date, he will receive the promised amount at once. If the date should happen to be further on, he must patiently wait till its arrival; but meanwhile he may count the promise as money, for the Bank is sure to pay when the due time arrives.[3]

An element of faith is required to walk into a bank, speak to the teller, and present a check. If you know that the bank's monetary resources are gone, you wouldn't bother even to walk into the bank.

"Some fail to place the endorsement of faith upon the check," Spurgeon continues, "and so they get nothing; and others are slack in presenting it, and these also receive nothing. This is not the fault of the promise, but of those who do not act with it in a commonsense, businesslike manner."[4]

Just as cashing a check takes faith, so does cashing in on a promise from God. You have to claim it like a check, only instead of taking it into your hand, you hold it in your mind and spirit by reading the Word of God. You mull over it, seeking its value and considering where in your life you can best apply it.

Look again at the promise at the beginning of this chapter. I can imagine what you might think when you read it. It might seem, in fact, like a huge slap in the face to hear God promising blessings and joy when one of your beloved children is diagnosed with autism.

And that promise may, indeed, seem worthless—unless the One who makes it is trustworthy. Can you trust God? Is He faithful to His promises? You may very well be angry at Him for allowing this to happen to your child, and I understand why you might feel that way. It is impossible to have faith in a promise—and by this I mean putting action to it, staking something of your life in it—if you have no faith that the promise maker will keep his word. In order to believe that a promise is true, you must have a relationship with the one who issued the promise in the first place.

So in the next chapter we spend some time with the Promise Maker.

We'll step back to an era long before the existence of autism, and ask, "Can I really trust a God who allowed this to happen to my child, and to our family?" and "Does God care about my child? I mean, really care?"

I will also tell you about the greatest Advocate my son has had or ever will have. This Advocate is ready to help your child, too. He is, in fact, thoroughly familiar with your case file and is waiting for your call.

Promise to Treasure

God's faithfulness

I'll never forget the trouble, the utter lostness, the taste of ashes, the poison I've swallowed. I remember it all—oh, how well I remember—the feeling of hitting the bottom. But there's one other thing I remember, and remembering, I keep a grip on hope: God's loyal love couldn't have run out, his merciful love couldn't have dried up. They're created new every morning. How great your faithfulness!

—Lamentations 3:19–23 (MSG)

Chapter 2

The Anchor of Our Lifeline

Learning to Trust and Obey the Promise Maker

What, what would have become of me, had I not believed that
I would see the Lord's goodness in the land of the living!
Psalm 27:13 (AMP)

You might be thinking, How can I trust God when He allowed my child to suffer with autism? Or maybe you're asking, How can I depend on a God who created a world that includes incredible pain and suffering? These are complicated questions, to be sure, and I can understand if you're asking them. The truth is, I've asked them myself.

Living with the reality of autism can make you feel like you're drowning. Desperate to keep your head above water, you grab hold of a lifeline. Can you rely, though, on who or what is on the other end of that line? You can—if you believe, claim, and live in the promises of God. In order to apply these promises to your life, however, you must have faith in the Promise Maker.

I was the first of our family to graduate from college, leaving my small steel town and moving to the big city. I always had big dreams, but motherhood was never one of them. It wasn't that I didn't want to hear the sweet voice of a child calling me "Mama," it was just that I hungered for so many other things first. But the years passed and I married my husband, Matt—which is another story of God's faithfulness in my life. Matt and I believed that God would let us know when it was time to make the move from being a couple to becoming a family. That heavenly nudge came in 1998, and soon I became pregnant.

When our daughter, Elise, was born, my outlook on life forever changed. Everything I'd valued before—all of my hopes, goals, dreams—were minuscule compared to the life-altering gift of motherhood. The axis of my world shifted, and I fell in love with being a mother while holding Elise.

My heart opened wide to every aspect of motherhood. When she became a toddler, I'd walk with her tiny hand in mine, pointing out every tree, bush, and flower on our way. Through her eyes I saw a different world, one of beauty and adventure that, at last, didn't revolve around me. And Elise has become a delightful girl. She's kind, compassionate, and inquisitive.

Although Elise had melted the walls of my heart to the adventure of motherhood, Alec was another story. When I realized that my son had developmental disabilities, I knew that I was the last woman on earth who could handle the responsibilities of raising a child with special needs. I just didn't have the strength for it. I didn't have the patience, the wisdom, or, quite honestly, the selflessness required to do it. I was well aware of my own limitations. I reasoned, *There are people whom God has put on this earth to rise to this kind of challenge, but I'm not one of them. Not me.*

Neither am I capable in this book or in my own wisdom to fully explain the theology about pain in the world. The good news is that we shouldn't hesitate to take our difficulties to God, even our most difficult queries. After all, John the Baptist did the same (see Luke 7:19). Trust me, God won't hit the "smite" button if we ask Him the tough questions. So in this next section let's explore why we can trust God even in a world full of suffering.

A World Without Autism: God's Original Plan

The Bible clearly tells us that God did not create this world to be a place of suffering. As detailed in the book of Genesis, He created it quite perfectly: "God saw all that he had made, and it was very good" (Gen. 1:31 niv). God's original design was a garden without autism or disease, without sorrows or tears.

He also gave man a costly gift: a free will. He did this because He longed for relationship with a people who wanted to be with Him. You see, our God is a gentleman. He never forces us into relationship with Him. God yearned for a people who would *choose* to love Him, desiring to be His people. After all, a forced love is not really love at all. We, however, took His wondrous gift of free will and used it to deny the very One who gave it to us.

When Eve and Adam ignored God's instruction not to eat of the Tree of the Knowledge of Good and Evil (Gen. 2:17), they actively turned their backs on God as their Lord. They had been warned that if they rebelled, they would die. Instead, they chose to do things their own way. That's when creation took a fall. Sin entered into God's perfection and changed everything, utterly polluting it.

The problem with sin is that it separates us from a holy and perfect God. As one drop of poison completely contaminates pure water, sin corrupted the whole of creation. God had to separate Himself from the sin, and from a sinful humankind. In addition He, as a Just God, had to provide a just penalty for sin:

To Adam, God said:

> The ground is cursed because of you. You will eat from it by means of painful labor all the days of your life. It will produce thorns and thistles for you, and you will eat the plants of the field. You will eat bread by the sweat of your brow until you return to the ground, since you were taken from it. For you are dust, and you will return to dust. (Gen. 3:17–19)

From this point in time and because of sin, the ground—that is, all of creation—was cursed. From then on, there has been hard labor in order to survive, thorns and thistles would result from our labor, and lastly, man would return to dust. Further, not only hardship, but disease had entered the world.

All this because of sin. Sickness and disease exist not because God "allowed" them, but because humans wanted to believe the lie that they could be like God. God is no more pleased with the current state of his creation than we are.

It may seem that God was overly harsh in providing such appalling penalties for sin. The judgments of God, though, reflect His great wisdom, even though they often don't make sense on the surface. But take heart, God did not leave us to die in the weed-infested garden. He couldn't leave us in a diseased world, forever separated from His love, any more that we could leave our child alone to suffer with autism.

In Genesis 3:15 God addresses Satan, who was in the form of a serpent: "I will put hostility between you and the woman, and between your seed and her seed. He will strike your head, and you will strike his heel."

Warren B. Wiersbe is a theologian and the former pastor of The Moody Church in Chicago. He has authored more than 150 books and is a respected writer of biblical commentary. Wiersbe's insights into Scripture are warm and easily understood, and he always emphasizes how to apply Scripture to life. In *The Wiersbe Bible Commentary: Old Testament*, he gives the following explanation of Genesis 3:15:

> God's words to Satan (v. 15) are called the "protoevagelium," "the first gospel," because this is the first announcement of the coming of the Redeemer found in the Bible. To God's old covenant people, this verse was a beacon of hope (Gal. 4:1–4); to Satan, it was God's declaration of war, climaxing in his condemnation (Rom. 16:20); and to Eve, it was the assurance that she was forgiven and that God would use a woman to bring the Redeemer into the world (1 Tim. 2:13–15).[1]

Even before God pronounced His words of punishment for sin, He proclaimed His plan for restoration and healing.

Parents, Jesus is the promised "seed" that would strike Satan's head. Jesus willingly came into our world and paid the price of our sin—a death sentence—though He did not sin. Even at the moment of punishment and separation, God revealed His plan for restoration and healing. *Jesus rescued us!*

He reached down from on high and took hold of me; he drew me out of deep waters. He rescued me from my powerful enemy, from my foes, who were too strong for me. They confronted me in the day of my disaster, but the LORD was my support. He brought me out into a spacious place; he rescued me because he delighted in me. (Ps. 18:16–19 NIV)

Scripture tells us, then, that before everything went wrong with the world, God already had His perfect plan prepared: He would enter our world in the form of His Son, Jesus, to bring us home.

A Purpose and a Plan

God has a special purpose and plan for you, as a parent, and for your precious child, too. That plan will not be hindered by autism. His plan is, in fact, to bless you and your child *through* autism! Sound impossible? To man, yes, but not to God. The apostle Paul confirms it: "And we know that in all things God works for the good of those who love him, who have been called according to his purpose" (Rom. 8:28 NIV).

Even now, God is weaving together his design for your tapestry, the colors, the thread, the pattern. He has carefully chosen materials that are proven for beauty and strength. Everything has a place in His design. He is clearing out any obstacles that would hinder the completion of this beautiful tapestry. Oh, what plans He has!

The much loved promise in Jeremiah 29:11 says, "'For I know the plans I have for you,' declares the LORD, 'plans to prosper you and not to harm you, plans to give you hope and a future'" (NIV). Take heart; God knows what He is doing! In God's hands, autism is only another beautiful fiber in the tapestry of colors for your life and the life of your child. He can take this disorder and weave it, like a vibrant thread, into something of beauty and grace and strength, a magnificent masterpiece of great worth and priceless value.

God Wove a Plan for Me

Often in the darkest of times, God sends someone to help us. To Matt and me, this was Susan Kincaid, a wonderfully warm woman with

a sincere heart for children. Susan was the director of the small preschool operated by Forest Hill Church in Charlotte, North Carolina.
She has the gift of seeing the best in the little ones she cares for at the
preschool. Her gentle direction and kindness created an environment
where I could literally feel the love when I walked through the door.

I discovered the preschool on September 12, 2001, one day after the
towers fell at the World Trade Center in New York City. Alec was only
a few months old. Elise, then two, was attending another local daycare
three full days a week so I could work part-time from my home as a
marketing consultant.

I'd decided against taking Elise to her daycare that day. Many
churches were hosting prayer vigils including my own, Forest Hill
Church. I wanted to go too, but with Alec so young, I didn't want
to potentially disrupt others in prayer by bringing young children.
Instead, I drove Alec and Elise to the small playground at the church
so Elise could play, Alec could sleep . . . and I could pray.

On September 12, 2001, I struggled with the brutal reality that
nothing about life is guaranteed. Would I be taken away from my family unexpectedly? With the future so uncertain, how could I protect
my kids and give them security? How could I ensure that my dreams
for my children would come to be?

I couldn't.

What I didn't yet know was that even those dreams, the dreams
every parent holds for his or her children, were not safe. The dreams
I had for my own son were soon to be, in fact, powerfully shaken and
tested.

But God was in that small playground, even in the cataclysmic aftermath of September 11, setting up the scene that would place people
in my life to help me. Even with the entire world in a state of upheaval,
His omniscient eyes were upon me—and my children.

As I sat on the park bench brooding about the many incidents of
the day before, a woman came out of the church leading a group of
children who looked to be Elise's age. The children joined Elise on
the playground and instantly welcomed her into their group. I silently
watched the woman as she looked after them. There was something

about her, a confidence and an air of patience and love that I had not felt in anyone at Elise's current daycare. There was something else, too, that I observed in this group of little children. Those kids were *happy*!

On recent afternoons I'd picked up Elise at her current daycare to hear reports of her distress over one issue or another. Teachers at the daycare were short-termers: they didn't remain on staff for long. Elise would come to love one teacher only to have her be gone the next day. It was a safe environment, but one that was constantly changing, and Elise craved stability. Over the previous weeks, I'd been having doubts about leaving her there. Was I doing the best for her that I could?

At the church playground, I began a conversation with the woman who introduced herself as Miss Robin. I questioned her about the preschool. Her words were encouraging, so I went in for a tour and that's when I met Susan Kincaid, the preschool director I admire and respect. Without any hesitation, she fit me into her busy schedule and walked me from room to room where I saw happy and contented children playing together.

That very day I enrolled Elise into an available slot, which, to my delight was in Miss Robin's class.

Once the transfer was complete and Elise was an official student, she blossomed. Elise loved the little school and so did I. She spent the following three years there, attending half days, four days a week.

When Alec was two, I naturally enrolled him there as well. That's when Matt and I first began to see that something was "different" about our handsome son. His behavior disintegrated into a series of tantrums, and his teachers were unable to handle him.

After a year of experimentation with different strategies to help Alec in the classroom, I found myself standing in the hallway outside of Miss Robin's classroom with Susan Kincaid. She had called to ask if I would meet her at the school to talk about Alec. With apprehension, I agreed.

At the time, Alec had just recovered from a second ear surgery. Surgeons had inserted yet another set of ear tubes to help drain excess fluid and prevent future ear infections. Matt and I were certain that Alec's difficulties—including those in the classroom—were the result of poor hearing and ear pain. This was also about the time that God had lifted the veil, and I'd recognized the troubled world in which Alec lived. Matt and I had hoped the second surgery would be the catalyst that would bring about success and we could all begin to reach him.

As I drove to the meeting, I held on to the hope that Susan would tell me that Alec's behavior was improving. But as I approached her in the school hallway, I caught a glimpse of her grim expression, and something thick and hard sank to the pit of my stomach.

"Kelly . . . Alec isn't doing better."

I stared at Susan, dumbfounded. She explained that she'd been observing Alec in the classroom and at play. He wandered around the room without engaging. He wouldn't transition from an activity without falling to the floor in a fit. Susan often had to remove him from the classroom to calm him down, fearing that he would injure himself during the episodes of fierce tantrums and head banging.

I waited for some word of improvement, but instead the news grew worse. Susan told me that Alec rarely interacted with the other children, preferring to play with a few Thomas the Tank Engine toys that he carried at all times. In addition, Alec rarely turned when his name was called, something I'd attributed to the ear infections.

But he's just difficult, I thought.

Susan spoke gently to me, explaining that Alec might have some developmental "problems" and may need some extra help to succeed. She knew of experts who could help. She suggested that Matt and I take him for an evaluation. It would be in his best interest to have some testing done to find out exactly what was going on with him. I thanked her, quite disingenuously, and told her we'd think about it.

I should have seen it coming—this unwelcome news from Susan. I'd been aware of Alec's troubles with transitioning for most of the year. On most days Alec refused to leave the classroom, forcing me to carry him out of the school, red-faced, tossed over my shoulder while he furiously beat on my back. Carrying my four-year-old daughter's crafts and drawings, two lunchboxes, and a kicking and screaming boy was cumbersome to say the least. I was humiliated and embarrassed as other moms walked hand in hand with their own well-behaved children, some sneaking sideways glances as we struggled along.

What must they think of us? I was certain they must have been thinking, *What a terrible mother. Can't she control her son?* Even worse was the possibility that they were thinking, *What a terrible child.* After a while I learned to be a few minutes late to the school so I could miss the other mothers and avoid their concerned stares.

Still, I knew in my heart that Alec was not really a "terrible" child. But at home, Alec's behavior had become more and more complicated. Getting him to do ordinary things was a struggle—leave home, come home, put on a coat, put on shoes, eat, start and stop, everything was hard. I chalked it up to having a difficult child. Elise, two years Alec's senior, was such a sweet and well-behaved girl that I honestly felt it was "my due" to have a difficult second child. Maybe God had given me an easy child first to prepare me for a tough child this go around.

These are the things we allow ourselves to believe. In a state of denial about possible reasons for my son's strange behavior, I clung to a myriad of excuses and rationalizations. When Susan mentioned that my son might have a developmental disability, walls of denial and anger rose within me. I wanted to hide behind these walls. *There's nothing "wrong" with our son!* I thought, refusing to consider that Alec had, as Susan put it, "developmental problems." *Maybe Susan just doesn't want the hassle of dealing with an unruly little boy. Maybe Miss Robin doesn't want a small bit of disruption in her classroom.*

Denial is a powerful thing. It led me into a new, gut-wrenching phase in the days that followed my conversation with Susan. I began incessantly analyzing everything my son did. I put Alec's every action, every sound (he wasn't speaking much), and each tantrum under my internal microscope, looking for ways to validate my need for Alec to be declared well and "normal."

Did you ever notice that sometimes God whispers the truth to us, even when we don't want to hear it? It's a voice that warns us when our child needs help, and a voice that demands our attention. Not long after my talk with Susan, I heard this voice. I was standing in my bedroom, watching Alec walk around the room, babbling incoherently. I called his name and he didn't respond. I called again, "Alec? . . . Alec!" Again, nothing. Suddenly, my eyes were opened and I saw clearly for the first time: *It's true. Something is wrong with Alec.* I fell to the carpet and wept. I knew. Susan was right.

God had placed Susan in my life for a reason. She had the strength to point out something I didn't want to see or hear. She encouraged me to get help for my son when I was in a state of denial. Because of Susan's willingness to confront me, Matt and I began an early intervention program with Alec, something we both believe was a crucial foundation for the improvement we later began to see in him. Susan set into motion a chain of events that enabled us to take immediate action to help Alec. Without her prompting, I have no idea how long we would have remained in denial.

Why We Can Trust the Promise Maker

You may want to believe God and His promises, but fear stands in your way. It's easy to trust something small to God, but we're talking about your child here! How can you trust God with something so dear to you?

Did you know that God cannot lie? The book of Hebrews explains it this way:

When God made his promise to Abraham, since there was no one greater for him to swear by, he swore by himself, saying, "I will surely bless you and give you many descendants." And so after waiting patiently, Abraham received what was promised.

Men swear by someone greater than themselves, and the oath confirms what is said and puts an end to all argument. Because God wanted to make the unchanging nature of his purpose very clear to the heirs of what was promised, he confirmed it with an oath. God did this so that, by two unchanging things in which it is impossible for God to lie, we who have fled to take hold of the hope offered to us may be greatly encouraged. We have this hope as an anchor for the soul, firm and secure. It enters the inner sanctuary behind the curtain, where Jesus, who went before us, has entered on our behalf. He has become a high priest forever, in the order of Melchizedek. (Heb. 6:13–20 NIV)

We can put our faith and trust in the promises our God makes to us. He is holy, and as such He cannot go back on His word. To do so would corrupt His holiness. "But I will not withdraw My faithful love from him or betray My faithfulness. I will not violate My covenant or change what My lips have said. Once and for all I have sworn an oath by My holiness; I will not lie to David" (Ps. 89:33–35). God is perfect, unchanging, and faithful. His Word is absolutely perfect and true, and history proves it. That's why we can trust His promises.

Jesus: The Key to the Promises of God

It's hard to trust a stranger. To truly trust God, you need to know Him; you must be in a relationship with the great Promise Maker, the Creator of the universe, the great I AM who always was, always is, and always will be. The only way to glimpse the Father and learn to walk with Him is first to know who Jesus is. Jesus says in the gospel of John, "If you knew Me, you would also know My Father" (John 8:19).

To know God, get to know Jesus, the perfect example of God's love for us. You can start by reading Matthew, Mark, Luke, and John, which relate in different accounts Jesus' time on earth, and find out what He was really like. Study Christ, His actions, His life-giving words, and the way He cared for those around Him. All sixty-six books of the Bible carry the same theme: God reaching out to man in need, and man finding God through Jesus. Beginning in the book of Genesis, Old Testament Scripture is filled with prophecies of Christ. In the text of the Gospels, we walk alongside of Jesus to witness an infinite God wrapped in flesh. The more you read about Jesus, the more you will know Him personally, and in doing so, you'll find Him true to His word. Don't take my word for it. Read about Jesus' faithfulness for yourselves.

Christ gives us the gift of knowing God! We can catch a glimpse of God's power, glory, and care as we read about Jesus traveling from town to town to reach out to the poor—touching them, healing them, empowering them, and proving their value in God's kingdom. Jesus, sometimes to the dismay of His disciples who wanted Him to hurry along, went out of His way to love those who were often overlooked by the public.

Don't allow anyone's example of Christianity to be a substitute for getting to know Jesus Himself! There's only one perfect example, and that example is Jesus alone. The rest of us are all merely works in progress. Get to know Jesus and you'll get to know the Father who has blessed His children with promises to rise above any situation in life—and, parents, that includes autism!

An Autistic Child's Greatest Advocate

Jesus is not only the key to knowing the Promise Maker, He is also the One who guarantees the promises of God. Parents, if we are to lay hold of those promises, we must know Jesus Christ, the One who signed them in His blood at the cross.

"Jesus told him, 'I am the way, the truth, and the life. No one comes to the Father except through Me'" (John 14:6). There's only one way to approach the throne of the Most Holy: you need to be in relationship with Jesus. Through Christ, and only through Christ, can we overcome this world's hardships—such as autism—and have the full right to a treasure of promises given to the children of God. Through Christ, we have access to God. We may walk with Him, sharing our hearts and needs with Him. We can boldly approach God without hesitation to ask Him to help us rescue our own children.

Right now, Christ, the greatest advocate any child with autism could ever need, sits on God's right hand. Because of Him, you can approach the Father as a trusting child approaches his or her daddy whenever that child has a need. There's no waiting list, no application form to complete. No appointment is necessary. He is waiting for your call, and He is willing and able to rescue your baby. God is ready at this moment to give you the help you need—but you will have to ask for it.

If you do not yet know Jesus, ask Him to come and be the Lord of your life. The Bible confidently proclaims, "If you acknowledge and confess with your lips that Jesus is Lord and in your heart believe [adhere to, trust in, and rely on the truth] that God raised Him from the dead, you will be saved" (Rom. 10:9 AMP).

Don't wait another moment! Get to know the Savior.

What It Means to Be a Child of God

So now you've been introduced to Jesus—if you didn't already know Him—the guarantor of God's great promises to believers. When we accept Jesus as our Savior and give our lives to Him, we become the very children of God: "But to all who did receive Him, He gave them the right to be children of God" (John 1:12–13). As such, we can lay claim to the promises of God.

Imagine the privileges you would have if you were a child of an American president. Just a drop of Daddy's name would open doors for you. Yours would be a privileged life, one full of opportunity and promise, all because you were a child of the Commander-in-Chief. Think of the government agencies that could help you navigate the difficult waters of autism.

Need a therapist for your son? No problem.

Need a doctor for your daughter? Here's a list of the top physicians in the nation.

Need some special financing to pay for their services? Just mention your daddy; his credit is more than good.

How, then, would you carry yourself? Would you look at your battles with autism in the same way? Would you feel overwhelmed and underresourced if you had access to the wealth of the White House? Would you be afraid of tomorrow? Or would you walk with your head high because you knew the power of your surname?

Although you don't have access to the White House and all of its privileges, through Christ you have access to even better: the very throne room of God as a child of God. All that is promised in the Bible, and it's yours. You *are* a child of the King!

When you surrender your life to Him, you are His, called by His name. With that name, you can now approach the throne of God in the full authority that Jesus gives you as a child of God. Take a moment to think about doing just that: close your eyes and envision approaching the holy throne of the Almighty—at the invitation of and authority given by Jesus. Hard to fathom, but it's true.

The writer of the book of Hebrews encourages believers to "approach the throne of grace with boldness, so that we may receive mercy and find grace to help us at the proper time" (Heb. 4:16). Child of God, put on your Christ-given robe of righteousness, the one that His sacrifice provides for you, and walk right up to the throne with all of the authority that Christ died to give you.

Remember that our great Advocate, Jesus, sits at the literal right hand of God and His eyes are on us! The Bible says that God has written our names on the palms of His hand (Isa. 49:16). God the Father and Christ the Son are not deaf to the cries for help from families dealing with autism.

Are You Ready to Trust?

You stand at a crossroads. If you're to have all that God promises, if you're to be all that God intends you to be, then you have to actively choose God's unique and, dare I say, privileged path. If, however, you are to receive the miraculous rewards God has planned for you and your child, you will have to submit to God, to His wisdom and authority.

Learning to walk with God starts with a choice. This is what it means to make Christ the Lord of your life. You must decide that you desire everything that He has for you. You have to be willing to step onto a road that is unfamiliar if He leads you to it. Sometimes He is going to take you where it might seem not the best way to go. But He knows the dangers that lie ahead on the more obvious route. You must be willing to take the risk and choose what seems like a detour because you know that's the way God wants you to go.

Do you trust God enough to jump into the depths of His promises? Are you ready for God to lift you above autism and give you a view of what lies beyond? It's a purpose and a plan for you, for your child, and for your family. It's a life of joy.

Have you arrived at a place in your battle with autism where you're ready to hand over the reins to God? Handing things over to Him doesn't mean, of course, that you won't have God-given tasks and responsibilities in caring for your child.

Many people learn to trust God only when they've come to a dead end in their lives and are without the strength or resources to go on.

That's the reality of human nature. Most people won't hand the reins over to God until their carriages are about to tumble off of a cliff. To find joy, however, the true joy offered to us as children of God, that's exactly what we must do: trust God to prevail over autism's grip on our families.

Parents, I must remind you again that God is a gentleman. He will come and inhabit our lives only if we invite Him. He never forces Himself upon us. But we can't lay claim to God's promise until we accept that we need His help to live above autism. We have to ask Him for help, and then submit by walking step-by-step down the path He shows us.

Do you really want God's help?

The next step will seem difficult—even incomprehensible—unless you know the never-ending compassion and love of Jesus.

Why Submission Is Necessary

It's time to submit to God's plan. But who enjoys being told to "obey" and "submit"? Our society hates these words. They do not evoke warm and comforting feelings. Our human nature hates submission. We have strong wills that demand to do as we please when we please, and to live life on our own terms.

If we're truly God's children, however, and in relationship with Him, and if we really want God's best for our lives, we must submit to His plan even if it doesn't make sense at the time. As we walk, we must trust that God knows what He's doing.

Why? One reason is that God sees the entirety of our lives at once, from beginning to end and beyond to eternity. We never know what lies just beyond the corner, but God does! He sees everything at once, every intertwining path of those around us, every obstacle to come. He knows our strengths and weaknesses better than we know them ourselves. As a shepherd leads his sheep away from danger, so God's Holy Spirit wants to lead us.

We say we love God, but do we trust Him enough to take His hand and, like a small child, go where He leads us?

> Some people were bringing little children to Him so He might touch them, but His disciples rebuked them. When Jesus saw it, He was indignant and said to them, "Let the little children come to Me. Don't stop them, for the kingdom of God belongs to such as these. I assure you: Whoever does not welcome the kingdom of God like a little child will never enter it." (Mark 10:13–15)

The kingdom of God is not a place in the distant future. In the Matthew 10:7, Jesus said, "The kingdom of heaven is at hand!" (AMP). He calls us to enter His kingdom today, surrendering every problem to His authority.

This includes our cares and concerns about autism. When you turn all of your cares about autism over to God, He does not let those concerns lie in a heap at His feet. No! Instead, He picks up the pile and begins to work in mysterious and wonderful ways until autism is no longer a burden to you. In this, God is glorified.

Spurgeon writes the following in *Faith's Checkbook*:

> What a joy to belong to a kingdom in which everything is being made new by the power of its King! We are not dying out: we are hastening on to a more glorious life. Despite the opposition of the powers of evil, our glorious Lord Jesus is accomplishing His purpose and making us, and all things about us, "new" and as full of beauty as when they first came from the hand of the Lord.[2]

Take a moment and chew on this: despite autism and even through it, God will accomplish His purpose in our precious children, making them as beautiful as when God placed them in our arms! Satan would have us believe that autism has lessened our child's purpose and ability to have a full life. This is not God's message, and He longs to prove this to you, but you must submit to His plan.

My Moment of Submission:
Calling Out to God for Help

When I was finally forced to accept that my son had autism, I was completely and entirely broken. Grasping the gravity of the situation, I took a mental inventory of my abilities as a mother and found a vast difference between what would be required of me and what I had to offer. I was in no shape to raise Alec and it terrified me. I was like an animal, backed into a corner, desperate in my own self-doubt.

It was simple: I just couldn't do it. I couldn't handle autism. I knew I lacked what it would take to raise Alec. That's when I knew where to go for help.

As a child I'd experienced God's faithfulness by trusting Him in little things. Over time I'd sought His help with substantial needs, from small problems—such as helping me find friends in school—to larger issues, such as directing me in my marriage and career. In every single instance, I'd found that when I sincerely sought God's direction, He provided an answer for me. Some of His answers had been immediate; others required me to wait. But always and without failure, God had answered my calls for help. So I desperately called out to the One who had never failed to be there for me. I could go to my Savior, my Deliverer.

On the afternoon when I called Alec's name repeatedly without getting a response, God gently broke through to me. He shoved aside my denial and showed me that something was, in fact, wrong with Alec. A strong wave of sorrow washed over me, and it forced me to my knees on the carpet of my bedroom: *I need You, God. I'm in a situation I can't fix. I can't do this. I need You to carry me through it.*

God was waiting for this moment. He heard my cry and He answered me. As the minutes passed by with me on the floor, another wave of sorrow washed over me. But as it receded—and it did recede—it took with it my fear of the unknown. I suddenly saw the mountain of autism in a new way, a mountain that could shift and topple with God's touch. It was a mountain that, with God's help, we could climb and move beyond.

God had awakened in me a new hope and determination to help my son. I had Jesus, and according to Scripture He is more than enough: "Whatever I have, wherever I am, I can make it through anything in the One who makes me who I am" (Phil. 4:13 MSG).

Submission Creates a Place for Miracles to Occur

Only by submitting to God's plan do we create a place in our lives for miracles to occur. Yes, miracles still happen today—they happen as God takes our greatest battles, surrendered to Him, and blesses us through them. This doesn't make sense in human terms, but God's ways are higher than we can understand. One kind of miracle is that He uses our trials and makes something wonderful with them, reinforcing our foundation of faith for future battles.

In *Faith's Checkbook*, Spurgeon eloquently explains the blessing that comes when we submit to God's plan:

> This is tantamount to a promise: if we will bow down, the Lord will lift us up. Humility leads to honor; submission is the way to exaltation. That same hand of God that presses us down is waiting to raise us up when we are prepared to bear the blessing. We stoop to conquer.[3]

Are you ready to take a chance to see what miracles God is preparing for you? Have you come to a point in your struggle with autism where you want to surrender your anxiety, pain, and sorrow to God so that He can make something good from this trial? No human can understand how it happens, but I promise you this: when you give autism to God, He will give you back something beautiful. That's His promise to you.

Don't wait another minute! Go to Him today with all of the authority you have as a believer in Jesus and a child of God. Pour out your heart to Him. Don't hold back a single detail. Let Him know your frustrations and your needs, and don't forget to let Him know if you are angry as well. He is a very big God. He can take it all—so don't miss out on what He waits to give to you by holding on to any of it. You can trust Him with every care.

Steps to Take to Build Your Faith

Now that you know the foundation for accepting, believing, and living in the promises of God, here are some steps that will help you make those promises a real, an active, and an integral part of your own life.

+ Keep a journal of what God is doing in your life. Record specific promises as you discover them in Scripture and note when they are fulfilled in your family life.
+ Post a different promise each week on your refrigerator. Memorize it and think about what the promise means to you at this time in your life. Use a Bible concordance to look up other verses and so you can study related text in Scripture that support and explain the promise.
+ Ask God to help you believe His word! (See Mark 9:24: "Immediately the boy's father exclaimed, 'I do believe; help me overcome my unbelief!'" [niv])
+ Look around for evidence of God's faithfulness in the lives of other believers. When you see God doing something special in their lives, ask them about it. Exciting confirmations of God's hand at work are seen every day in the lives of those around us. Remember to look for God's fingerprints around you and make a note of them.
+ Don't forget to thank God for each fulfilled promise in your life. Stay close to God by reading Scripture and by praying with thanksgiving. As Psalm 140:13 says, "Surely the righteous will praise Your name; the upright will live in Your presence."

I'm so excited to tell you about the inheritance that God has provided in His Word for His children! In the following chapters we'll look at just a few of these promises and how, by trusting them, we can soar above autism and find the joy God wants us to have!

Promises to Treasure

Joy, peace, hope

May the God of your hope so fill you with all joy and peace in believing [through the experience of your faith] that by the power of the Holy Spirit you may abound and be overflowing (bubbling over) with hope.

—Romans 15:13 (amp)

Competence

We have this kind of confidence toward God through Christ: not that we are competent in ourselves to consider anything as coming from ourselves, but our competence is from God.

—2 Corinthians 3:4–5

Caring and blessing

Humble yourselves therefore under the mighty hand of God, so that He may exalt you in due time, casting all your care upon Him, because He cares about you.

—1 Peter 5:6–7

Chapter 3

The Blessings Behind
the Giants
God's Promise of Blessings

*So I said to you: Don't be terrified or afraid of them! The
LORD your God who goes before you will fight for you, just
as you saw Him do for you in Egypt. And you saw in the
wilderness how the LORD your God carried you as a man
carries his son all along the way you traveled until you
reached this place.*

DEUTERONOMY 1:29–31

I've often referred to our struggle with Alec's autism as a struggle against a giant. It's the struggle for language and social skills; the struggle to obtain proper therapists, specialized education, and funding; the struggle to meet dietary restrictions and needs. The list can go on and on.

It's also been a struggle for me to reach Alec on his own terms. Some say that we just need to accept autism. I'm a mother who accepts *Alec*. Autism is a condition that impairs a child's ability to interact with the world around him or her. I am not willing to let that be without a fight. I want to do as much as I can to treat Alec's autism in order to help him live and function in this world. I've always known that there is a promised land for Alec. I know that he is God's unique and valued son and that he can face the giant of autism and overcome it.

Another young boy, a shepherd boy, once took only what he had and faced a giant. The boy ran full force at the most fearsome enemy of Israel and overcame him, and I know Alec can overcome his giant, too. Why? Because no giant—whether a taunting, armor-clad enemy, or a life-changing diagnosis of autism—can stand against God's will for us and His present help when we call.

Boy Meets Giant: How to Face Autism

In 1 Samuel 17, the young shepherd boy, David, is sent to deliver some food to his brothers in the army of King Saul. When he gets there, he finds the entire army and King Saul shaking in fear because of a Philistine warrior named Goliath:

> A giant nearly ten feet tall stepped out from the Philistine line into the open, Goliath from Gath. He had a bronze helmet on his head and was dressed in armor—126 pounds of it! He wore bronze shin guards and carried a bronze sword. His spear was like a fence rail—the spear tip alone weighed over fifteen pounds. His shield bearer walked ahead of him.
>
> Goliath stood there and called out to the Israelite troops, "Why bother using your whole army? Am I not Philistine enough for you? And you're all committed to Saul, aren't you? So pick your best fighter and pit him against me." (1 Sam. 17:4–8 MSG)

King Saul is a tall man himself, but this aggressive giant intimidates him to the bone. For forty days, every soldier in that army has listened to the taunts of Goliath. No one is willing to stand up to him and defend Israel, the people of God.

No one, that is, but David. He's different. He understands that the giant is the enemy of not only the Israelite people, but the enemy of God—because the Israelites are God's people.

Incredibly, instead of fearing Goliath as King Saul and the other soldiers do, David reacts in anger: "Just who is this uncircumcised Philistine that he should defy the armies of the living God?" (1 Sam. 17:26). David is astounded that no one will stand up to Goliath.

David knew something that King Saul and his entire army had for-gotten: the battle was not theirs to fight alone. In reality it was God's battle. David believed this truth with every ounce of his being, and he was willing to stake his life on it. Although his own father did not deem David worthy of serving alongside his brothers in the army, God chose this boy to bring down the Israelites' most fearsome enemy.

David grabs what he has on hand, five small stones from a nearby stream and, in all of the authority of God, runs at towering Goliath, shouting,

> You come against me with a dagger, spear, and sword, but I come against you in the name of the LORD of Hosts, the God of Israel's armies— you have defied Him. Today, the LORD will hand you over to me. Today, I'll strike you down, cut your head off, and give the corpses of the Philistine camp to the birds of the sky and the creatures of the earth. Then all the world will know that Israel has a God, and this whole as-sembly will know that it is not by sword or by spear that the LORD saves, for the battle is the LORD's. He will hand you over to us. (1 Sam. 17:45–47)

I get chills when I read David's words to Goliath. Did you catch his determination and his declaration that the battle was God's? When David defeated the giant, God was glorified in the presence of King Saul, the Israelites, and the Philistine army. Young David, who came at Goliath in the name of God, had prepared for the victory by declaring for all to hear that this battle was not his battle, but God's. Therefore, the resulting victory ensured that no one would ever doubt that God's hand brought down Goliath.

Oh, how often God uses men and women whom the world over-looks to carry out His mightiest of works! God wants to fight for us in our battle with the giant of autism. Never forget that we were created to glorify God, and He wants to be glorified in our victories when we've stood up to autism and overcome it.

The Battle Belongs to the Lord!

When the giant first came to call on my family, for a while I couldn't make a move against it. I was immobile, quaking in my boots as the giant laughed and told me that our family was powerless against it. That is, until I finally understood that this battle was not really my own, nor was it my family's.

As discussed in the previous chapter, believers are God's children, His own people. As such, our fight with autism is very important to God. Don't allow the voice of the Enemy to taunt you, telling you that God doesn't care about your struggle with autism. Declare the battle as God's, grab what resources you have, and run at the giant with courage. You are simply human, and so you are powerless to defeat such a giant, but you can be strengthened in knowing that God is well equipped to bring down your giant.

When our family chose to declare our clash with autism as God's battle, it was like a key that opened all of the power of Heaven. Here are some ways you can apply that power for your family.

Pray Away the Armor

Goliath's armor bearer stood between the giant and David. What's standing in your way in your struggle to help your child? Is it a monetary need for therapies? Social acceptance? The loss of communication? Help for education? Chronic illnesses or the loss of hope? If you truly know the One who stands to help you, like David, you have no reason to let these pieces of armor hinder you. Pray them away in the name of the Lord. Know that He is able to dismantle every one—no matter how thick or formidable—that blocks the way of your child becoming all that God intends him or her to be.

You might pray by using David's battle cry from 1 Samuel above, but make it apply to your particular need, something like this:

> Father, we're facing financial struggles right now as we're trying to overcome autism. The need for money is a barrier that comes against us. But we face that barrier in the name of the

Lord, because we are Your children, so that barrier defies not
only us; it defies You, our Father. I pray that You will strike
down that barrier, and we will let everyone know that we have
a God, and they will know that this battle was won by the
Lord. In Jesus' name, amen.

Do not let all those barriers cause you to doubt. Causing us to doubt
God is a tried but true tactic that Satan uses because it works for him.
As a believer, you are God's chosen child and He stands with you. "Call
on Me in the day of trouble; I will deliver you, and you shall honor
and glorify Me" (Ps. 50:15 AMP). He loves to be glorified through the
victories of His people!

Give the Best You Can and Trust God to Multiply It

When you ask God for help, He *will* help you, but that doesn't mean
that you won't have work to do. God wants us to put action to our faith.
David didn't just stand in the battlefield and wait for Goliath to get
struck down by a lightning bolt from heaven. He picked up what was
available and ran into action. Five small stones don't seem like much
use in battle against a giant, but God was pleased to use such meager
weapons to win the victory.

Matt and I don't have unlimited financial resources to help Alec.
We've done the best we can, but more specialized care and treatments
are available than we've been able to provide. I trust that God will take
what Matt and I give to help Alec—our financial resources for therapies, educational assistance, biomedical doctors and medicines, and
most of all, our compassion and love—and will multiply it so that Alec
will have all that he needs to be the man God intended him to be.

Grab your five small stones! Don't get discouraged about all that
you wish you could do, but can't. Instead, look around you and see
what monetary and personal resources you do have, and use them to
provide the best therapies you can to help your child. And then ask
God to bless the therapy time. Ask Him to supplement what you can
provide with God-given resources. He could place a wise parent in
your path who has been around the autism block a few times and who

can offer priceless advice to you. Perhaps He will line up a teacher for your child who has a unique gift of working with children with autism.

Educate Yourself

That first summer after Alec's diagnosis, I was like a sponge soaking up all the autism books and Internet sites I could find. I purchased a handful of books from the autism section of our bookstore and, on my lunch hours, devoured everything I could about autism. Each day I'd grab one of my books and head for my favorite taco joint, Moe's, where I sat by myself, turning page after page, dunking chips in salsa, and crying more than a few tears. I must have been a sight to see, sobbing over my salsa! But I learned so much about autism in this way. (I also learned about the therapeutic power of chips and salsa!) Ask God to guide you to the right sources of information and advice. He certainly tossed a few great titles my way (see appendix B).

Seek Support

Ask everyone you know to pray for your child, and ask God to guide you to people who can provide support and information. Then get out there and join an autism support group such as the Autism Society of America, Generation Rescue, Autism Speaks, the National Autism Association, Defeat Autism Now!, or Talk About Curing Autism. (Contact information for these and other organizations is in appendix B.)

By polling parents of older autistic children, we were able to find doctors gifted in the autism field. We acquired initial medical testing and attended one of the Autism Research Institute's "Defeat Autism Now!" conferences.[1] These conferences provide information about biomedical supplements and therapies to reduce the symptoms of autism so that a child can focus, communicate, and learn. Using the information we gained, Matt and I soon began to see dramatic improvements in Alec's behavior and ability to communicate.

Offset Finances

Matt and I were not able to afford thirty or more hours per week of Applied Behavioral Analysis (ABA) therapy, but we could afford ten hours a week.[2] We were then able to put in some additional hours ourselves after attending a few seminars to learn how to do so and after working with Alec's educational therapist.

When Alec was four, Matt and I enrolled him in a private school with an excellent autism program, but after one year (and one refinance of our home mortgage), our financial reserves were gone and we couldn't afford to enroll Alec in the school for the following year. I was apprehensive about pulling Alec out of private school and enrolling him in public school.

Then I remembered that God's provision is alive and well in public schools as well as private schools. I took a deep breath and started praying for God to provide for Alec in the public school system. With that prayer, Matt and I got busy to help Alec make the transition.

We set up an appointment with the public school principal and staff, sharing with them our concerns, hopes, and dreams for our son. We assured the principal that we wanted to work with the educational team to provide the best possible education for Alec. We offered to assist the school in Alec's education any way we could, and offered to volunteer there. Because we expressed our concerns in a nonaccusing way, the school administrators were more than willing to work with us.

The result? God blessed—and multiplied—our efforts. He lined up wonderful teachers to work with Alec. He even placed several wonderful kids in each classroom who befriended Alec and helped him to grow socially as well as intellectually. In the following year, Alec made significant advances and surpassed our expectations educationally, socially, and emotionally. Each year, we meet with teachers and staff, pray, and reap the blessings of watching Alec grow.

Parents, God will work in His way to provide for your child in any setting. So do the very best you can and trust God to multiply it. Matt and I didn't accept defeat when we could no longer afford an expensive private school with an autism program. We knew that God promised to supply for Alec's needs—even in a public school. The private school Alec attended is exceptional, but we shouldn't limit God's ability. He can work in more than one setting. He promises to continually provide for Alec—and your child—each year. In chapter 11, I'll talk in greater detail about God's promise of sufficiency and how we can count on Him to provide for our children.

Our Reason to Persist and Prevail: The Blessings Behind the Giants

Do you feel sometimes weighed down in caring for your child? Do you sometimes wake up in the morning, still tired, and want to throw in the towel? Are you weary from the responsibilities of raising a child with an autism spectrum disorder? Do you feel that the responsibilities of raising a child with special needs is more than you can endure? Let me share with you another Bible story that encourages me when I feel like that. It's found in Numbers 13.

With a mighty hand, God has brought the Israelites out of Egypt. Now it's time for their first look at the Promised Land after leaving their lives of slavery. Moses sends scouts, one man from each of the twelve tribes of Israel, into the new land to bring back reports of what they see.

The scouts find clusters of grapes so large it takes two men to carry one on a pole between them! They find pomegranates and figs and, indeed, a land flowing with milk and honey. The land is all that God promised.

But they also see giants in the land.

Caleb, one of the scouts, tries to encourage the people to go at once to take the land. He believes that God will help them conquer it just as God had promised them. But the other scouts who went with him, except Joshua, answer, "We can't go up against the people because they are stronger than we are!" (Num. 13:31). And they spread discouraging reports about the land among the Israelites:

> The land we passed through to explore is one that devours its inhabitants, and all the people we saw in it are men of great size. We even saw the Nephilim there. (The offspring of Anak were descended from the Nephilim.) To ourselves we seemed like grasshoppers, and we must have seemed the same to them. (Num. 13:32–33)

For a long time I felt like a grasshopper in the shadow of the fear-some giant, Autism. We received a few discouraging reports of our own, especially a particularly depressing one from a local neurologist. Matt and I had read about the tens of thousands of dollars per year it takes to treat a child with autism, and we didn't have piles of cash lying around or even stored up in the bank. We didn't have any rich relatives standing by ready to write a check for us to get Alec started in an ABA therapy program.

But we did have a sincere desire to help our son. We were willing to do whatever we could with what personal resources we had to bring him out of the world of autism to communicate with the world around him. Matt and I knew that God was on our side and that He would help us.

After scouting the Promised Land, Caleb also knew that God was with the Israelites. He knew God was bigger than the giants, so he encouraged the people to take the land. But the people wouldn't be-lieve him. Because of their doubt, that generation never made it to the Promised Land. They didn't believe God's promise that He would give this rich land to them. Instead, they focused only on the giants.

There were great blessings to be had behind those giants, and God's full intention was to empower the Israelites to conquer the giants and have the blessings. Likewise, God has prepared great blessings for you and your child. But you'll have to trust Him to conquer all that stands in the way of your reaching those blessings.

At times, the obstacles will seem greater than you can endure. Some days will be overwhelming. Your resources may be very low. Know, however, that God often shows His glory most clearly when our situ-ations seem most desperate. On your dark days, do not focus on the giant before you. Instead, focus on the God who is with you.

In our family's struggle with autism, every day I'm faced with a choice: Do I focus on the autism, or on the beauty of my child? Do I focus on the giant or on God's promises for our kids? Oh, God has such wonderful promises for our children!

Parents, I can't tell you what blessings are behind your personal gi-ants. But I can tell you that the blessings are worth the battle. Press on, dear ones. Don't give up when the situation seems hopeless. Remember, the battle is God's. He will help you pierce the armor of and conquer the giants in your life. "But let all who take refuge in You rejoice; let them shout for joy forever. May You shelter them, and may those who love Your name boast about You" (Ps. 5:11). He has already promised you the land; now you must claim it in the name of the Lord.

The Blessings Behind Alec's Giants

After we moved Alec to the public school, Matt and I were concerned that he might have to repeat kindergarten—but we were wrong. He not only passed kindergarten, he passed at the top of his class academically! As of the writing of this book, Alec has completed first grade, again at or above grade level academically, in a typical classroom. My boy is on his way to second grade!

Matt and I often ask ourselves, "What it is that has worked?" Was it the early interventions? The behavioral therapies? The biomedical therapies? Matt and I believe that Alec was greatly helped in receiving an early diagnosis so that we could begin an early intervention program. We also believe that the ABA therapy and verbal behavioral therapies have worked for Alec. In addition, the biomedical treatments have been a key reason our son is doing well.

But I believe that the single greatest resource responsible for Alec's improvement is God. He has, is, and will be there for us, and He loves Alec and has promised to help him. If all we could afford to give Alec was love, then God would see to it that love was all Alec would need to be all that He intended Alec to be. So we've given Alec our best, knowing God has done the same.

So I have to thank Him.

Parents, remember that each autistic child is different. Therapies that work for one child do not always work for another. I encourage you to research the available autism treatments and decide the best way to treat your child. Above all, don't lose hope. Seek God's promises and believe them.

And don't let anyone tell you that the giant will win.

There is joy in every day when we look for it. Even on the hardest days, I've found new wisdom in understanding Alec. I thank God for this boy—for all that I learn through him, for the miracles he shows me daily, for the smiles that warm my heart, because I know they came with a price of many hours of hard work, time, and tears. My son has worked incredibly hard for every smile.

The greatest blessings are behind the biggest giants in our lives. With the resounding "THUD!" of each defeated giant, God is glorified! With God's help, those giants will fall. Believe it, because our kids are so worth our best efforts. It's all about faith, hope, and love. But the greatest of these is love.

Promises to Treasure

God is on your side

You grumbled in your tents and said, "The LORD brought us out of the land of Egypt to deliver us into the hands of the Amorites so they would destroy us, because He hated us. Where can we go? Our brothers have discouraged us, saying: The people are larger and taller than we are; the cities are large, fortified to the heavens. We also saw the descendants of the Anakim there."

So I said to you: "Don't be terrified or afraid of them! The LORD your God who goes before you will fight for you, just as you saw Him do for you in Egypt. And you saw in the wilderness how the LORD your God carried you as a man carries his son all along the way you traveled until you reached this place."

—Deuteronomy 1:27–31

Victory in the battles

Yet amid all these things we are more than conquerors and gain a surpassing victory through Him Who loved us.

—Romans 8:37 (amp)

A life for your child

This day I call heaven and earth as witnesses against you that I have set before you life and death, blessings and curses. Now choose life, so that you and your children may live.

—DEUTERONOMY 30:19 (NIV)

Power in weakness

But He said to me, "My grace is sufficient for you, for power is perfected in weakness." Therefore, I will most gladly boast all the more about my weaknesses, so that Christ's power may reside in me.

—2 CORINTHIANS 12:9

Chapter 4

The Dawn Will Surely Come

God's Promise of Refreshment and Renewal

*And how blessed all those in whom you live, whose lives be-
come roads you travel; They wind through lonesome valleys,
come upon brooks, discover cool springs and pools brimming
with rain! God-traveled, these roads curve up the mountain,
and at the last turn—Zion! God in full view!*

PSALM 84:5–7 (MSG)

It's July 13, a sticky, humid day in Charleston, South Carolina. The air is heavy and oppressive as Matt and I walk alongside Alec and Elise through the old city market. Here, we pass rows of vendors, and women who are weaving low country grasses into elegant works of art.

It's been a long day. Matt and I had decided to break up the monotony of summer by taking a three-hour drive to Charleston for this spur-of-the-moment family getaway. Trips like these are like rolling the dice. Sometimes they work and everyone has a good time. Other times, we wind up wishing we'd never left home.

Today, the heat is soaring in the old city nestled on the South Carolina coast, and the air is thick like molasses. Our shirts are sticking to our backs, and our feet are sore from walking miles across the historic downtown. Even so, it's been a good day. We began with a tour of the Battery, where a delighted Elise stretched her arms wide to support several cooing pigeons. We walked uptown and jumped onto a crowded carriage tour, a big gamble with Alec's inability to hold still. Matt and I took turns holding him as the tour guide pointed out architectural and historic details of the city. I was nervous that Alec might disrupt the tour and throw a tantrum, but things had gone surprisingly well.

It is now late afternoon and we're thirsty, sticky, and tired. The kids are fussy and it's time to think about heading home. We weave our way through the grid of streets toward Charleston Harbor on our way back to the Battery where the BGV—our Big Green Van—is parked. On the way, we walk alongside the historic harbor and arrive at Charleston's Waterfront Park on the Cooper River. In the heart of this park is Vendue Plaza, and there we discover a breathtaking fountain, a perfect circle of water jets spewing from stone cylinders positioned around its circumference. The water glistens as it shoots skyward and then arches back to the earth, meeting in the center and pouring over smooth, blue paving stones.

Darting in and out of the water jets are children of all ages, boys and girls escaping the heat. As we approach, Alec's eyes light up and he runs for the cascading streams. He's now able to tolerate shoes, and I catch up to him to wriggle them from his feet. When he is at last free, he dashes into the oasis of cool, refreshing water.

I'm filled with the sound of Alec's rolling laughter. It's contagious, and soon we're all laughing, taking off our shoes and joining him in the fountain. The water, seeming to have a life of its own, invigorates us. With the rushing of the water, the heat is forgotten. We are refreshed and renewed again.

I have a picture of this precious moment, of Alec and the fountain. He's squatting to touch the cool water with his fingertips, laughing in delight. The crystal streams are gushing over his little bare feet, lapping at his blue shorts and sprinkling his polo shirt. What a beautiful reminder to me of *living water*, the gift that Christ offers us as believers.

Water: The Difference Between Life and Death

Think about it: water carries life; it bubbles and flows. Its oxygen replenishes, it washes away our thirst and the dirt of the day. It restores our fading energies, allowing us to go farther than we could without its life-sustaining properties.

Life cannot exist without water. Without it we become parched. We dry up, our skin hardens and our tongues thicken in need of moisture. Our bodies shut down and eventually, if left without water, we will die.

In Scripture, God uses springs and fountains of water to illustrate His ability to restore His life within us, enabling us to carry on with the work He calls us to do. In biblical times when water was often scarce, a fountain of water was not simply a refreshing treat to play in on a hot day. It was the difference between life and certain death.

Refreshment for Hagar

The book of Genesis includes the account of Hagar, a distraught woman fleeing across the desert. Let me set up the biblical story while you strap on Hagar's sandals to walk a little of her journey and discover how she came to this desperate situation.

In Genesis 16, Abram's barren wife, Sarai, is impatient. She makes the choice not to wait any longer for God to fulfill His promise to her husband that she would bear him an heir. Sarai decides to give God a little hand by encouraging Abram to take her handmaiden, Hagar, as an additional wife for the purpose of bearing Abram an heir. Abram agrees, and Hagar becomes pregnant. Naturally, the tension begins to build between Sarai and her servant, Hagar. Knowing that she is carrying Abram's child, Hagar becomes haughty and begins to despise Sarai in her heart. Sarai, angered by Hagar's attitude, does what any wife might do and blames poor Abram (who never should have listened to Sarai in the first place) for the discord in their home.

When Sarai complains to Abram about Hagar, he takes the easy way out and tells Sarai in verse 6 to "Do with her whatever you think best" (NIV). What Sarai thinks best is to mistreat Hagar. And so the pregnant Hagar chooses to run away, heading for her old life in her former land of Egypt and away from the hardships of her situation in Abram's house.

God, however, had a different plan for Hagar and for her yet-to-be-born son. The story continues as God sends the Angel of the Lord to her, finding her beside a spring in the desert on the road to Shur (Gen. 16:7–11). The angel convinces her to return and submit herself to her mistress, Sarai. He offers a wonderful gift as well: a special promise that she, too, would have descendants too numerous to count. She would give birth to a son and name him "Ishmael," which means "God hears."

In God's perfect timing, He honors His promise to Abram and Sarai. He first changes Sarai's name to Sarah, "lady, princess, queen," and Abram's name to Abraham, "father of multitudes." Then the aging Sarah is blessed with her own son, Isaac (Gen. 21:1–3). But trouble is brewing in Abraham's tent! One day, Sarah catches Ishmael mocking her son, Isaac, after Abraham had prepared a great feast in celebration of Isaac. Protective of her son and angry, Sarah bitterly complains to Abraham, "Drive out this slave with her son, for the son of this slave will not be a co-heir with my son Isaac!" (Gen. 21:10).

Poor Abraham is distressed. He gives Hagar a small amount of food and a skin of water for the journey and sends her on her way. So it is that we once again find Hagar on the run, but this time she has her son Ishmael to care for on the journey.

Hagar and Ishmael are now alone in the heat of a desert with just a little food and Abraham's small skin of water. Imagine how Hagar must have felt, unsure of her future and the future of her beloved son? She must have felt anxious and totally forsaken in that wilderness without direction or a plan. I imagine she had a bit of self-pity as well, and perhaps anger. After all, Ishmael's conception was Sarah's idea.

Hagar was no doubt hungry, thirsty, and hot. I can see her giving the last droplets of water to her son, the water that meant life for both of them. And with that, she came to the end of her ability to care for her son:

> When the water in the skin was gone, she put the boy under one of the bushes. Then she went off and sat down nearby, about a bowshot away, for she thought, "I cannot watch the boy die." And as she sat there nearby, she began to sob. (Gen. 21:15–16 niv)

As a parent of a child with autism, have you ever felt like Hagar? Do you ever want to throw your hands up in defeat? Have you ever wanted to give up?

Hagar has nothing left. She has no hope remaining. She's helpless to ease her son's suffering. But in her distress, she does not cry out to God for help. She was a woman who had personally met with the Angel of the Lord! And yet, she is so focused on the bleakness of her current situation that she forgets to look up for help.

Although we don't always feel it, God's help is always close. He waits for us to surrender and call out for help. His heart leans down to the brokenhearted, and when a child is hurting, rest assured, God is well aware of it. His ear perks up when He hears a child sobbing. Scripture says that "God heard" the boy crying and responded swiftly. Once again, God sends His angel to minister to the desperate mother:

> God heard the boy crying, and the angel of God called to Hagar from heaven and said to her, "What is the matter, Hagar? Do not be afraid; God has heard the boy crying as he lies there. Lift the boy up and take him by the hand, for I will make him into a great nation." Then God opened her eyes and she saw a well of water. So she went and filled the skin with water and gave the boy a drink. (Gen. 21:17–19 NIV)

The requirements of taking care of an autistic child can often outweigh your personal resources, just as the sustenance Abraham gave to Hagar and Ishmael was not enough for the enormity of their needs. The unpleasant truth is that our own resources, too, have limits. Even with the aid of governmental support, therapies, and—if we're lucky—monetary assistance, we have no assurance that these things will help our child overcome autism. But take heart, because God's resources have no end! They are limitless! When the resources we are offered through the world don't meet our needs, take heart in knowing that God promises to provide for our needs (Matt. 6:28–34).

And know this: God hears the cries of our autistic children. He does not turn a deaf ear to their needs. He knows exactly where we are in the desert of autism and He is waiting for us to cry out for renewal and refreshment. The loving God who refreshed Hagar and her son with life-giving water promises to provide the life-giving spring of water we need to sustain us.

Warren W. Wiersbe provides an encouraging insight regarding Hagar's story:

> So often in the trials of life we fail to see the divine provisions God has made for us, and we forget the promises He has made to us. We open our hands to receive what we think we need instead of asking Him to open our eyes to see what we already have. The answer to most problems is close at hand, if only we have eyes to see (John 6:1–13; 21:1–6).
>
> Hagar is certainly a picture of the needy multitudes in the world today: wandering, weary, thirsty, blind and giving up in despair. How we need to tell them the good news that the water of life is available and the well is not far away (John 4:10–14; 7:37–39)! God is kind and gracious to all who call on Him, because of His beloved son, Jesus Christ.[1]

The Holy Spirit: Our Living Water and Advocate

Jesus knows that caring for a child with autism can deplete one's strength. He knows the responsibilities are great and often thankless. He knows that the heaviness is real, just like the heat of a July day in Charleston. As we wander through the days taking care of our children, our energy dwindles until we reach the point when we just can't give anymore. It's a dangerous place to be, because in our tiredness we often take out our frustrations on those we love. May the Lord forgive me for the many times I've snapped at my children or my husband when my internal gauge was on empty.

When I feel I've reached the limit, so often the voices in my head turn negative. My focus shifts from Christ to my own inabilities. *I can't do this.* I feel overwhelmed and I wallow in self-pity. *Why does our family have to go through this battle? I never asked for this!*

In times like these, it's important to remember that Christ never meant for us to go it alone. He promises to give us living water to sustain us:

Whoever drinks from the water that I will give him will never get thirsty again—ever! In fact, the water I will give him will become a well of water springing up within him for eternal life. (John 4:13–14)

John Wesley, Christian theologian and early leader of the Methodist Church, in his *Notes on the Whole Bible* gives the following notes about Jesus' promise:

[He] will never thirst—will never (provided he continue to drink thereof) be miserable, dissatisfied, without refreshment. If ever that thirst returns, it will be the fault of the man, not the water. But the water that I shall give him—The spirit of faith working by love, shall become in him—An inward living principle, a fountain—Not barely a well, which is soon exhausted, springing up into everlasting life—Which is a confluence, or rather an ocean of streams arising from this fountain.[2]

Just like a spring of water, God's restorative love flows through a person filled with the Holy Spirit. This is the fountain Christ offers us. In layman's terms, possessing the gift of the Holy Spirit means having God with us at all times. It means we always have the assurance of the One who stands with us to help us overcome autism.

This incredible, life-sustaining gift came at a great cost to God. The Spirit is a sacred gift given after the great sacrifice of Christ, who perfectly atoned for our sins. Because God is and will always be holy—pure, clean, perfect, and without blemish—and man is sinful, there was no way for God to be with us. That is, until Christ came to cover our sins with His priceless blood, atoning for every sin we have committed and ever will commit. The great work of Christ is complete and never needs to be repeated. Because of Christ's covering our sins, and His gift of the Holy Spirit, we have strength from Someone living in us, strength that those living without Christ do not have access to.

I cannot fully express how invaluable the Holy Spirit is when caring for a child with autism. Because of this incredible gift of God, we now have the presence of One with the highest credentials, One who knows everything there is to know about our situation. The Holy Spirit knows more about autism than the brightest of scientists or therapists. There are no doors that our heavenly Companion cannot open. You won't get put on a waiting list to reach Him. He doesn't require insurance, and there are no deductibles. He is working twenty-four hours a day. In fact, even as you sleep, this Advocate is on the case! He is far greater than autism, and promises that if we trust Him, we will be blessed and strengthened in spite of it.

This is what Christ says of the Holy Spirit:

> But the Counselor, the Holy Spirit—the Father will send Him in My name—will teach you all things and remind you of everything I have told you. . . . When the Counselor comes, the One I will send to you from the Father—the Spirit of truth who proceeds from the Father—He will testify about Me. (John 14:26; 15:26)

The Greek word Christ uses in these verses for "counselor" is *parakletos* (par-ak´-lay-tos) and it means "an intercessor, consoler, an advocate, comforter."[3] Christ sent the Holy Spirit to be our personal Advocate to assist us on earth. Not only that, but Christ Himself is also our heavenly Advocate, interceding for us at the throne of God.

Do you realize what this means to us as we struggle with autism? When the world is shorthanded in terms of answers and resources to help our kids, think of the overflowing provisions we have via the Spirit and Christ, our Advocates. Chew on that truth a moment or two.

In chapter 12 we'll discuss the secret to living an abundant life, regardless of any situation, by staying within this never-ending fountain of living water.

For Refreshment, Open Your Eyes and Look Up!

Although there is no cure at this time for autism, the condition does not prevent God from reaching our children. He calls us to open our own eyes, just as He opened Hagar's eyes. He challenges us no longer to fear that our children won't get all that they need to survive autism, but instead to take our child by the hand and cry out to Him for help. Lean on your Advocates to carry you through dry spells and bring to your tired soul a bubbling, invigorating fountain. Open your eyes and look for a renewal of spirit—the refreshing spring of water God sends so we will know that the hand of the Lord is with us.

By providing for us and our autistic children, the Lord is glorified as the world sees Him dismantling barriers that seem insurmountable:

> The poor and the needy seek water, but there is none; their tongues are parched with thirst. I, the LORD, will answer them; I, the God of Israel, do not forsake them. I will open rivers on the barren heights, and springs in the middle of the plains. I will turn the desert into a pool of water and dry land into springs of water. I will plant cedars in the desert, acacias, myrtles, and olive trees. I will put cypress trees in the desert, elms and box trees together, so that all may see and know, consider and understand, that the hand of the LORD has done this, the Holy One of Israel has created it. (Isa. 41:17–20)

Take heart, parents! God hears our cries. He will provide resources for us in places that have no apparent help for autism. He will do amazing things to meet our needs, and in doing so, He will be glorified.

Promises to Treasure

God hears the brokenhearted
The righteous cry out, and the LORD hears,
    and delivers them from all their troubles.
The LORD is near the brokenhearted;
He saves those crushed in spirit.
Many adversities come to the one who is righteous,
    but the LORD delivers him from them all.

—Psalm 34:17–19

God will satisfy for eternity
But whoever takes a drink of the water that I will give him shall never, no never, be thirsty any more. But the water that I will give him shall become a spring of water welling up (flowing, bubbling) [continually] within him unto (into, for) eternal life.

—JOHN 4:14 (AMP)

Help from the Spirit for believers
He who believes in Me [who cleaves to and trusts in and relies on Me] as the Scripture has said, From his innermost being shall flow [continuously] springs and rivers of living water.

—JOHN 7:38 (AMP)

Renewal in the desert
The poor and the needy seek water, but there is none; their tongues are parched with thirst. I, the LORD, will answer them; I, the God of Israel, do not forsake them. I will open rivers on the barren heights, and springs in the middle of the plains. I will turn the desert into a pool of water and dry land into springs of water.

—ISAIAH 41:17–18

Rejoicing
They will come and shout for joy on the heights of Zion; they will rejoice in the bounty of the LORD—the grain, the new wine and the oil, the young of the flocks and herds. They will be like a well-watered garden, and they will sorrow no more.

—JEREMIAH 31:12 (NIV)

Hope for your child
For I will pour water on the thirsty land, and streams on the dry ground; I will pour out My Spirit on your descendants and My blessing on your offspring.

—ISAIAH 44:3

Support

[There is] a river—its streams delight the city of God, the holy dwelling place of the Most High. God is within her; she will not be toppled. God will help her when the morning dawns.

—PSALM 46:4–5

Chapter 5

Revelations Without Words

God's Promise to Reveal Himself

At that time Jesus said, "I praise you, Father, Lord of heaven
and earth, because you have hidden these things from the wise
and learned, and revealed them to little children. Yes, Father,
for this was your good pleasure."

MATTHEW 11:25–26 (NIV)

Bedtime prayers.

I love to spend the last waking moments of my children's day at the side of their beds. Listening to a child's sweet soliloquy, to which the audience is God Himself, I'm struck with the beauty and simplicity of these prayers that we, as adults, often lose. These bedtime prayers are sacred moments, a mystery uniting God with parent and child. Parents of neurotypical (nonautistic) children assume these sweet, innocent prayers are a guaranteed benefit of parenting. But to parents of children with autism who have lost their language, spoken words of prayer are to be treasured.

My own parents divorced when I was eight years old. I remember my mother crying in the bathroom, and the sadness that filled the rooms of our home. I do not hold any bitterness or regret for those difficult years of loneliness, bewilderment, and pain. My parents were, after all, doing the best that they knew how to do at the time. God, though, gave a gift to me from those uneasy days, because during this time I learned the value of prayer.

As my secure world fell apart, I turned to God with the simple faith of a child, praying in the night and asking for help. The memories of those whispered prayers are still with me, and have taught me that prayer is simply a conversation with the Father.

I was too young to know the significance of the various names for Jesus, and certainly too young to understand the meaning of the name "Immanuel" (God with us), but God revealed Himself as Immanuel to me. As my own parents' attention turned inward while they struggled to pick up the pieces of their own shattered dreams, God was there with me, holding my hand and providing a sense of supernatural peace. I can now even thank my parents for this head start in my prayer life. We were all in pain, but that pain taught me to pray.

It was only natural, then, that I yearned to share these special moments of prayer with my own children. Knowing firsthand the peace found in trusting God, and having spent years seeing God answer prayers in breathtaking ways, my heart burned to teach my own children about God's love and faithfulness.

I wanted to teach them about prayer.

Speaking in the Language of a Sponge

One of the most frustrating characteristics of autism is that it affects the ability to speak and process language. Like an invisible wall, autism is a barrier that inhibits our child's ability to communicate with us.

For Alec, the process of learning to speak has been agonizingly slow. He began by memorizing scripts from cartoons and favorite television shows and then repeating the scripts incessantly. This action is called "echolalia," and a friend of mine calls it "functional scripting." Matt and I just call it "robo-talk."

Alec used his memorized phrases whenever he was in a situation similar to the character in the show. For example, rather than saying "I'm hungry, Mama. What can I eat?" he would use a phrase right out of SpongeBob's mouth, exclaiming, "I want a crabby patty!" The tone of his words would lilt up and down, reminding me of a leisurely drive over hilly farmland. Although his speech was odd, I was thankful that he was talking at all.

During one family outing to a crowded Shoney's restaurant, my husband was asking Alec a number of questions to encourage him to talk. Alec was wearying of this game, and he wanted his daddy to stop asking him questions. To accomplish this end, he pulled from memory a script spoken by Squidward, the grouchy character in the SpongeBob cartoons. Alec turned to his father and said, quite loudly, "Daddy, go be stupid somewhere else!"

Let me tell you . . . forks dropped all over that restaurant when the other customers heard Alec talk to his father this way. They must have been shocked when we didn't discipline our son for being so rude. Actually, we were excited that Alec had exchanged "SpongeBob" for "Daddy." Matt and I could only laugh, because we knew exactly what Alec really meant to say. We knew he was tiring of mining for words so he could answer his daddy. As you're probably discovering, parents of autistic kids have to learn to speak many languages: Thomas the Tank Engine, SpongeBob, VeggieTales, and many others.

Revelations at the Bedside

It's been easy to pray with my daughter, Elise. At three years of age, I gave her a book of Bible stories written for preschoolers. Every night, we'd read a few stories and then discuss them together. Then we'd say prayers, with me marveling at the easy way she spoke to the invisible Creator of the Universe.

But with Alec? At three years of age, he had just learned to say "Mama." He did not comprehend my words and barely made eye contact. He never sat still. We longed to say prayers with our son, but he wasn't able to break apart the memorized scripts to formulate his own unique sentences. If Matt or I asked Alec a question that required more than a yes or no, he couldn't answer.

How could Alec, with these limitations, understand the abstract concept of prayer? However could I explain spiritual matters to him? Would he ever understand such things? I dreamt of a future when Alec and I would engage in deep conversations about God and ponder the mysteries of the universe. But Alec couldn't talk about concrete objects, let alone spiritual matters.

Many nights I sat at Alec's bedside and begged God to help me tell

Alec that God loved him. I wanted him to experience the peace and wonderment in knowing that God was a prayer away, with strong invisible arms waiting to hold him. I wracked my brain, trying to conceive a way for Alec to know how to pray to a God he didn't even know existed.

Oh, how little I knew!

A cartoon series helped to educate me. My son loved the animated VeggieTales characters and their series of videos. Everywhere Alec went, he carried the plastic versions of the VeggieTales heroes, Bob the Tomato and Larry the Cucumber. Woe to us if we ever left the house without Bob or Larry. One tantrum later, we'd turn around and head back home to fetch the tiny members of our family.

So in looking for a way to connect with Alec about God, I chose a simple song of prayer from the VeggieTales series, the "Thankfulness Song":

> I thank God for this day,
> For the sun in the sky,
> For my mom and my dad,
> For my piece of apple pie.[1]

Alec loves music, so I sang this same tune to him every night, praying that somehow, he would understand its message. One night as I sat down at his bedside to begin our nightly routine, Alec, in his typical few words, said to me, "Sing your prayer."

Those three words brought tears to my eyes, because I'd never called this simple song a "prayer," nor, for that matter, had I even mentioned prayer to my son! How could my autistic son, whose language delay was significant, understand that this simple song was a prayer? I don't know, but he did.

I'd had it all wrong. I was trying to do what only God can do: reveal Himself to Alec. I saw that God would reveal Himself to my son, just as He did to me so long ago. God promises to reveal Himself in His own timing and in His own perfectly matchless way: "At that time Jesus said, 'I praise you, Father, Lord of heaven and earth, because you have hidden these things from the wise and learned, and revealed them to little children'" (Matt. 11:25 NIV).

I cling to this verse from Matthew as Alec grows. God is fully capable of communicating with our children, regardless of their speech abilities. God will reach out to my son and embrace him. He will reach out to your child, too.

God proved this again to me another night at Alec's bedside. I whispered to him, "Mommy loves you, Daddy loves you, Elise loves you." Then, as an afterthought, I asked, "Alec, who is Jesus?"

I didn't think that Alec was yet able to discuss the concept of Jesus, whom he could not see or touch in a physical, concrete way. But to my amazement, Alec replied, "Jesus loves me."

Jackson's Extraordinary Prayer

Jill Urwick is the mother of Jackson, a handsome and engaging boy. His ASD symptoms have dramatically reduced after using the Defeat Autism Now! protocol.[2] Jill is one of the autism moms that I classify as a "warrior mom." She goes beyond helping her own son, working night and day to provide information and hope to parents of all ASD children.

Jill established a Verbal Behavior Inclusion program in the local public school system.[3] She also served as Director of Projects for Defeat Autism Now! for four years, and in 2002 she founded S.T.A.R. Parents (Seeking Treatment and Recovery), a proactive support group for North Carolina parents of autistic children. Recently, Jill founded Vital Interventions Accessible, an organization dedicated to making safe and effective interventions and therapies more accessible to families of children with disabilities.[4]

Jill shared a special story with me about one of Jackson's bedtime prayers. It's an extraordinary account of an extraordinary God whose love is not limited by autism. The following incident and its aftermath are told in Jill's own words:

> I used to worry about Jackson's ability to understand God's love, to the point that I would cry myself to sleep at night.

However, God, as He always does, showed me in such a powerful way that He was in control, and that, if anything, I should learn from Jackson and his ability to communicate with God in ways I couldn't even fathom.

We say prayers each night before bed. One night, about three years ago, when Jackson's speech was almost 100 percent delayed echolalia [scripted speech from cartoons] with virtually no conversational skills, we were saying prayers. Jack had learned a "rote" prayer, a simple one that we had made up.

But that night something was different. We had planted a garden about a week earlier, and Jackson was very interested in it. I said my prayer that night as always. And then I said to Jack, "Okay, it's your turn."

He began, "Dear Jesus," then there was a rather long period of silence. I asked him if he was done, but he said, "No." Then all of the sudden, he said, "Yes," followed by silence. Then, "No," and more silence. Then "Oh, yes," followed by silence, and then, "green beans, zucchini, cucumbers, peppers, tomatoes, watermelon, and cantaloupe." With tears streaming down my face, I realized he was having a conversation with God!

There was another long silence. I asked if he was done. Again, he said, "No," followed by another pause, and then, "Yes . . . I love You, too. Amen."

Jackson may not have been able to have conversations with *me*. But, more importantly, he was able to communicate with God Almighty!

In total amazement, I asked Jackson who he was talking to. He said, very emphatically, "God!" I asked, "Could you hear him?" He said, "Yes!" At that moment, I decided that if Jackson *never* had a real conversation with *me*, it was okay, because he was communicating with God on levels that most of us will never be able to attain. He could *listen* to God—the area most people struggle with!

As the nights passed, his prayers did seem to go back to the same little rote prayer. But, occasionally, he would say something to the effect of, "Please God, take this mercury out of my body!"[5]

A short time after that, I was able to share with Jackson about Jesus dying on the cross. He listened very intently, almost as if he knew already. He prayed, thanking Jesus for what He had done for him, and asked Him to live in his heart forever. Immediately after that prayer, Jackson screamed out, "I'm FREE! WOW!!!"[6]

Jill's skepticism caused her to doubt whether such a young child could truly understand salvation, so she took Jackson to see their pastor. After speaking with Jackson, whose conversation skills with people were greatly limited, their pastor was certain that Jackson had encountered God and that he did understand the concept of salvation.

Jill believes that ASD kids are communicating with God much more than we realize and on deeper levels than we can imagine. "That's where I find my comfort," she says. "Even when I can't reach Jackson, I know that God can. He is with Jackson always, even into the depths of autism!"

Jill hopes other parents are encouraged by Jackson's prayer story. "We have so much to learn from our little autistic children," she says. "God is going to work wonders through them! Even though their communication is very limited with us, we should never underestimate how God is able to really speak to their hearts."[7]

In Jeremiah, God asks, "Can anyone hide in secret places so that I cannot see him?" (Jer. 23:24 NIV). God can reach us anywhere and at any time. He is quite capable of revealing Himself to autistic children.

Speechless Revelation

Communication comes in many forms other than speech. A facial expression, a touch—all things can help us communicate with our children. Nonverbal children such as those with autism or other speech disorders learn to communicate in many ways.

God also speaks to us in many ways. His fingerprints abound in nature, for example. Standing at the seashore, you can feel His breath in the wind as it touches your cheek. On a moonless winter night, you gaze at starlight emitted eons ago, and in the silence you can almost hear His song of creation. Even the trees stretch up their arms in praise to the Creator.

God doesn't need words to prove that He exists. Centuries ago, when King David was a young shepherd boy, he walked alone in the night, gazing up into the darkness to take in the glory of God's night sky—and found Him there. Psalm 19 says of the heavens, "Day after day they pour out speech; night after night they communicate knowledge. There is no speech; there are no words; their voice is not heard. Their message has gone out to all the earth, and their words to the ends of the inhabited world" (Ps. 19:2–4).

In Isaiah, the seraphim, too, reinforce God's revelation in His creation: "Holy, holy, holy is the LORD Almighty; the whole earth is full of his glory" (Isa. 6:3 NIV).

Revelation by the Holy Spirit

Oh, God desires for us to know Him! We were, in fact, created to know Him and to glorify Him. He longs to take us under His wing and call us His children. He created us magnificently, wonderfully, in the secret places before we were touched by the world around us. His desire to be known by your child is real, and this desire is not lessened by your child's autism.

Second Peter states, "He is patient with you, not wanting anyone to perish, but everyone to come to repentance" (2 Peter 3:9 NIV). It does not say, "God wants everyone *who can* to come to repentance and salvation." Paul writes, "God's readiness to give and forgive is now public. Salvation's available for everyone!" (Titus 2:11 MSG). He doesn't say, "Salvation is available for *those who are able* to hold their own at a table discussion with the world's most knowledgeable theologians." No . . . The word *everyone* tells us that God's heart is for all of humankind, despite age, race, sex, education, economic status . . . or the state of the neural system.

I cannot verify this, but I believe that God has a special place in His heart for autistic kids. God understands them when the world cannot.

He understands their singsong speech—when they have it—and their gestures when they do not have speech. His Spirit works deep within their little bodies, touching their spirits, speaking to them in their silence, without words or audible language.

Through His Holy Spirit, God reveals Himself to us. This truth is confirmed in a discussion between Jesus and Simon Peter, recorded for us in Matthew's gospel:

> When Jesus came to the region of Caesarea Philippi, He asked His disciples, "Who do people say that the Son of Man is?" And they said, "Some say John the Baptist; others, Elijah; still others, Jeremiah or one of the prophets."
>
> "But you," He asked them, "who do you say that I am?"
>
> Simon Peter answered, "You are the Messiah, the Son of the living God!"
>
> And Jesus responded, "Simon son of Jonah, you are blessed because flesh and blood did not reveal this to you, but My Father in heaven." (Matt. 16:13–17)

No one told Peter that he was walking with the Messiah, the very Son of God. Yet, despite the differing opinions of the public, he knew the truth: he was in the presence of the Christ. As Jesus confirmed, God revealed this truth to Peter, not his own weak flesh and blood.

Parents, God will reveal Himself to your precious child as well!

God in the Darkness: The Story of Helen Keller

Helen Keller writes, "The best and most beautiful things in the world cannot be seen nor even touched, but just felt in the heart."[8]

Helen Keller, blind and deaf from infancy, rose above her lack of sight and hearing to profoundly impact the lives of others in miraculous ways. In Keller's book *My Religion*, she tells her story of seeking the Creator at an early age.

> As a little child I naturally wanted to know who made everything in the world and I was told that Nature (they called it

Mother Nature) had made earth and sky and water and all living creatures.[9]

This satisfied her for a while, but the observant Helen—who was possibly underestimated in terms of her ability to understand spiritual issues—sensed several troubling limitations in the Mother Nature theory. The more she considered nature, the more she was puzzled by the order and sequence of events in nature, its destructive forces and never-ending succession of seasons.

She writes, "Somehow I sensed that Nature was no more concerned with me or those I loved than with a twig or a fly, and this awoke something akin to resentment."[10] Even at such a young age, Helen knew there must be more to the story of how everything came to be. She turned away from the concept of Mother Nature and began inquiring about God.

Helen went to her teacher, Anne Sullivan, for answers to her spiritual questions about God and Jesus. According to Keller's great-grandniece, Keller Johnson-Thompson, Miss Sullivan took the inquisitive Helen to see Bishop Phillips Brooks, a greatly beloved theologian of the time and writer of the hymn "O Little Town of Bethlehem." Johnson-Thompson is often asked to tell a particular story from Helen's early years, involving her questions of Bishop Brooks:

> Anne Sullivan felt that if anyone could answer Helen's questions in a simple and beautiful way, Bishop Brooks could. Bishop Brooks understood Helen. He put her on his knee and told her in the simplest way that God loved her and every one of his children. He made him seem so real that Helen said, "Yes I know him, I just had forgotten his name.[11]

God had, indeed, revealed Himself to Helen even before she knew His name.

As the years passed, Helen's faith grew. Her lack of sight and hearing didn't stop her from heroically living out a divine purpose. She was able to rise above her physical limitations and change many lives. Through her writings, her impact on the world is impressive even today, years past her death in 1968. In the later years of her life, she wrote the book *My Religion* to share her faith with others.

Helen's story is but one example of God's reaching out to our children despite their physical handicaps or disorders. I'm convinced beyond a shadow of a doubt that God reaches out to all of us, despite darkness, silence, sensory overload, lack of language, situational hardships, or inability to communicate with others.

The bottom line is this: God reveals Himself to us in a special way that He specifically designs to reach us wherever we are. His message of love is written across the heavens. If we can't see that, it's also found in the sounds of creation around us. If we cannot hear this music, His existence can be found in the warmth of the sunlight on our skin, or in the embrace of a loved one. And somehow, when we are alone and silent, His inaudible words speak to our hearts, calling us to Him and telling us that we are, indeed, vastly loved.

> They took away what should have been my eyes
> (But I remembered Milton's Paradise)
> They took away what should have been my ears
> (Beethoven came and wiped away my tears)
> They took away what should have been my tongue
> (But I had talked with God when I was young).
> He would not let them take away my soul:
> Possessing that, I still possess the whole.
>
> HELEN KELLER[12]

....

PROMISES TO TREASURE

God holds your child

"I prayed for this boy, and since the LORD gave me what I asked Him for, I now give the boy to the LORD. For as long as he lives, he is given to the LORD." Then he bowed and worshiped the LORD there.

—1 SAMUEL 1:27–28

Strength and courage

Haven't I commanded you: be strong and courageous? Do not be afraid or discouraged, for the LORD your God is with you wherever you go.

—Joshua 1:9

Chapter 6

Making Sense of a Confusing Disorder

God's Promise of Wisdom

I have been driven many times to my knees by the overwhelming conviction that I had nowhere else to go. My own wisdom, and that of all about me, seemed insufficient for the day.

ABRAHAM LINCOLN

It's an understatement to say that autism spectrum disorders are bewildering. The very nature of a spectrum disorder is its many variations in symptoms, and degrees of autism from one child to the next. The differences from child to child are baffling. Some children are only slightly impaired, suffering only a few symptoms such as an inability to focus or a social impairment. Others are profoundly affected, not able to speak and constantly require intense care and supervision. As the saying goes, "If you've met one child with autism . . . you've met *one* child with autism."

One of the strangest and most confusing things about ASDs is the day-to-day variation of symptoms affecting a single child. There are wonderful days, now that Alec is older, when he can function normally and his autism is perceptible only to a trained eye. Some parents who've met Alec on a good day are surprised to learn that he *has* an ASD, because he functions and interacts very well. On those days I can rest a bit, and I'm excited by his progress. The mountain seems to be smaller than ever before and I can see the summit above me.

But every so often Alec has what I call an "off day," when certain immobilizing symptoms of autism return with a vengeance. On those days the progress we've fought so hard to achieve seems to vanish. On those days it's so hard to identify what's going on with my son.

Keeping my finger on what's going on with him biomedically is crucial, since his gluten-free, casein-free, and soy-free diet—and any occasional infraction of it—has such a dramatic effect on him.[1] At first he'll become irritable. He'll throw a tantrum, something he used to do many times a day but now does only on rare occasions. His language will be garbled. He'll slip back into "robo-talk," or echolalia (the compulsive repetition of a script from a source such as a book, computer game, or television show). He may spin or be hyperactive.

On Alec's off days, school is more difficult. His ability to focus will diminish and his eye contact will decrease. I may get a note from the teacher about a tantrum at school. Getting Alec to complete his homework on days like this is a feat. I'll find myself asking him the same question several times in a row before I get an answer from him. During these laboriously long homework sessions, I often end up popping a couple of aspirin to ease the headache that usually follows.

I can get so discouraged as I watch Alec temporarily lose some of the wonderful advances he's worked so hard to achieve. But the most discouraging thing about the off days is that I miss my son. I miss his playful interaction with me, and getting to see who this little guy really is.

Alec's off days throw me off, too. It takes me some time to realize what's really going on with my son: he's not simply misbehaving; he's acting out of frustration over his loss of lucidity.

A Tale of Two Potties

When Alec was about four, he was having a bad night while going through the bedtime routine. One clue that he's having an off day is a return of obsessive-compulsive behaviors. He'll be repetitive in his actions, often requiring a specific order to cope. This is a common symptom among children with autism. Parents of autistic children need to become adept at deciphering their child's rigid and sometimes unspoken requirements. You may, for example, have to sit in the same seat when driving in the car or when eating at the dinner table. Should you switch your typical seat, your autistic child is overwhelmed with distress.

On this particular night, Alec was agitated because his sister, Elise, was on the potty in their bathroom. Normally, this isn't a problem, but for some reason her occupation of this most important seat was interfering with his routine. On this night he could use no potty but *his* potty, and Alec wanted full and immediate rights to that potty. He wailed and fussed for his sister to move, but she was, unfortunately, having her own "potty moment" at the time. Elise, who at age six was well versed in "strategic autistic combat," called in her reinforcements.

So Matt and I joined forces, attempting to persuade our son to surrender his assault on my daughter's personal space and retreat to the toilet in our bathroom. I marched into the kids' bathroom, retrieved a kicking and screaming Alec, and took him to our bathroom. He loudly protested for a long while, outraged at his forced exile. After what seemed like an eternity, he finally raised a white flag and "did his business," albeit reluctantly. I carried him back to his room and tucked him into his bed, his blanketed fortress, and pulled the sheets up around his shoulders.

But the battle was not over. When Elise finally left the bathroom and retired to her bed, Alec insisted on going to the potty again— this time on *his* potty. I allowed him to do that, tapping my foot as I waited outside of the bathroom door for Alec to complete his mission. I tapped a long, long time. Finally, he trudged out and I put him back into bed.

I sighed with relief as I pulled the covers back up to his chin. But no! My son was not ready for surrender. Grabbing my hand, he cried, struggling with the words. He wanted to go back to his potty again! Apparently, my little man needed to spend more quality time on his special bathroom seat. Exasperated, I let him go back to the treasured potty and gave him all the time he needed. Minutes stretched on and on until my tired little son opened the bathroom door and finally allowed me to put him to bed for a third time. He was still crying as I tucked my little warrior back into his bed.

Sitting at his bedside, I saw waves of frustration crossing his face. He was struggling to find the words to say something to me, something that appeared to be of utmost importance. He was weeping and breathing hard, so I couldn't understand his words. I'm sure you know how incredibly frustrated I feel when I can't understand my child when he's desperate to communicate with me.

At long last, he calmed down enough and whimpered, "Mama . . . Mama . . . Mama . . . I'm . . . I'm . . . I'm . . ." He sobbed a bit more and finally managed to say, "I'm . . . I'm s-s . . . s-s . . . I'm . . . sorry . . . Mama."

Out of this long battle over two potties, we both had found victory. My little son, Alec, had never told me or anyone else that he was sorry. Oh, occasionally I'd prompt him to apologize for some infraction, but he'd only repeat the words after me. I was never sure he understood what he was saying. But that night my little man had been gripped by obsessive compulsion and was well aware that he'd caused a measure of distress. So for the first time, Alec wanted to apologize on his own, even though it wasn't necessary. As my little boy told me how sorry he was, I sensed the sadness in him. We both sat on his bed, hugging, crying together until a strange peace descended on us, and my Alec drifted off to sleep.

The truth was that Alec couldn't help his behavior that night. Somehow he was locked into it as if forced to go through a script of behaviors. On good days, Alec couldn't care less about which potty he uses, so I was blindsided that night by his obsessive insistence for his own potty. I hadn't noticed the subtle clues that Alec was having an off day. If I'd picked up on the signs earlier in the evening, I might have been able to prevent the battle entirely. Possibly I could have structured the bedtime routine so that Alec could have completed each task without hindrances. Unfortunately on this day I didn't see the clues until we were gridlocked in an exhausting battle.

All children misbehave and need redirection at times. How can we tell when our autistic children are misbehaving and when they're simply acting out of frustration because their lucidity is gone? How can we discern when they need discipline and when they're having an off day and need a little more understanding? Truly, our need for wisdom is great.

Wisdom to Discern Behavior

Symptoms of autism vary so greatly from child to child. How, then, can parents hope to understand the disorder or know how to help their child overcome it? Even more puzzling, how can parents understand where their child stands emotionally and physically at any given moment, when the symptoms of autism change from day to day, hour to hour, and even situation to situation? Even those in the medical profession are baffled over the puzzle of autism. What's a parent to do?

We need a supernatural ability to break into our child's world when autism blocks our way. We need a God-given instinct to decode autism's many mysteries, so we can meet our children where they are and help them be all that they are meant to be. Here's the good news: God is waiting to help us do this very thing!

Did you know that God promises to give us wisdom if we simply ask? God's promise of wisdom is an often-overlooked tool in God's box of promises that will help us understand our child.

Look at these verses:

> Now if any of you lacks wisdom, he should ask God, who gives to all generously and without criticizing, and it will be given to him. But let him ask in faith without doubting. For the doubter is like the surging sea, driven and tossed by the wind. (James 1:5–6)

God's desire to grant us wisdom is apparent and uncomplicated. There is nothing obscure or confusing about it. Everyone can use a stiff dose of wisdom each and every day, and in this promise, God offers to give it to us, no questions asked. When was the last time you asked God to grant you wisdom in a situation? If your answer is, "not today," then you're missing out on a valuable part of your inheritance of promises. God wants to give wisdom to us on a daily basis.

There are days when I simply don't know how to be the mom that my boy needs. There are days when Alec's behaviors and needs baffle me, and I have no idea what he requires of me. But do you know what? God knows. At any given moment and in any situation, God knows my child thoroughly, right down to the nucleus of each cell in his body. God knows what tensions my son faced at school today, what troubles will come his way tomorrow, and how to rise above each one. He knows what skills and resources I possess to guide my son through difficult situations. He knows what is going on inside Alec's little body when illnesses have invaded and he must visit the doctor. God knows my son, and God knows me.

When I find that Alec's autism has led me to another brick wall, I must remember to ask God for a dose of His infinite wisdom. In doing so, I remind Him of the promise to grant it to me and I thank Him for His knowledge of all things. I ask and trust God to be the unchanging and faithful God that He is, true to every one of His promises.

How many times have I forgotten to ask God for help to understand what's going on with my son? I become entrenched in whatever the struggle might be in a particular moment, and exasperate myself trying to fix the problem myself. I forget that God's desire, His will, is for me to be the best mother I can be for my son, and that He wants to help me. I just have to remember to ask!

Parents, it's imperative that we ask for God's wisdom to help us understand our children. We can avoid so many battles if only we remember to walk up to God's throne in the name of Jesus and ask for His wisdom. It's as simple as this:

> Father, my child is very troubled today, and I want to help him, but right now I don't know how. Please give me wisdom to understand what is going on and the patience to wait for Your answer. In Jesus' name, amen.

I find that when I do this, I'll have a new awareness of what my son needs. As understanding seeps into my soul, I receive a quiet knowledge of how to handle a situation.

Sometimes wisdom comes immediately. It may come as an "aha" moment, such as the time God showed to me that my son had a developmental disability. On that day understanding came in a single moment, and suddenly I could "see" my son clearly.

On some of Alec's off days, it takes time for me to catch on to what's going on with him. Initially it seems as if he's just being obstinate. Then I'll see a loss of clarity creep over his face. His frustration swells inside him, as if he realizes the loss and he's angry about it. Then God will give me an "aha!" moment and I'll remember that Alec has eaten something he shouldn't have, or I find that a supplement is not quite right.[2] Sometimes, I discover something at school has caused him distress.

Sometimes I might wait days for the understanding to come. There's no promise that God's wisdom will come immediately. You see, God dishes out His wisdom in His own time. But rest assured—His promise to give wisdom is good and He will be faithful to it. Waiting, though, takes patience—so ask Him for that, too!

As James 1:5–6 instructs us, ask in faith and do not be "driven and tossed by the wind." What does it mean to be "tossed by the wind"? Imagine a leaf being tossed here and there as the wind carries it. The leaf has no ability to choose its own destination but merely reacts to the wind, as if a victim to it. God doesn't want us to be like a leaf on the wind, swept away by our situations in life. He calls us to be more than conquerors, not victims! (See Rom. 8:37 NIV.)

Wisdom to Make Good Choices

There are so many theories, methods, and techniques that might help our children. Some will work well, others won't. There are numerous brilliant and talented physicians, teachers, and therapists who have a sincere desire to help our children. Such people have given their lives to helping those who suffer from autism. But be aware—there are also wolves circling our camp. They smile and offer promises to desperate parents in exchange for some hard-earned money. They prey on our desperation, sniffing it out, taking advantage of our need for hope. Their hearts are not for our children but for their own profit.

How can we know what therapies to pursue for our children? Which therapies are best for their unique needs? How can we know who has our children's best interests at heart, and who only hungers for a profit? The only way Matt and I have been able to make these decisions is to ask God for wisdom—and then wait for it.

Keep in mind that, currently, no specific protocol works for treating every child with autism. I can tell you that Alec has seen tremendous progress utilizing Applied Behavioral Analysis (ABA), as well as bio-medical methods such as a gluten-free, casein-free, and soy-free diet. Matt and I are amazed at Alec's progress, but we remain in need of daily wisdom to keep Alec on the road to recovery. As you do your homework and research therapy options, don't forget to ask God for daily wisdom to discern what is best for your child.

That wisdom, in the form of God's Spirit, dwells deep within be-lievers. If we just lay aside our own self-will, God offers wisdom to help us identify where to go to get our children the help they need. He helps us to make sound decisions for our kids, to discern the truth from fiction, and lead us away from the sharks who do not truly care about our children. God's wisdom is like a silent whisper that helps us understand our children, pulling back the veil so we can see them with God's own eyes.

Wisdom to Care for Your Child

God placed your child in your care for a reason. He trusted you enough to give you the mind-boggling responsibility of rearing not just any child, but a special child, one with a unique set of needs and a di-vine purpose. Perhaps knowing that *God* gave this task to you doesn't make it feel any less impossible. But take heart: you are not the first person to feel overwhelmed by your God-given task.

When King David's son Solomon took the throne of the nation of Israel, he was overwhelmed by the enormity of the call to rule over God's people. Solomon felt ill equipped for such a tremendous task. Even so, he knew that God had given it to him. Greatly concerned about the magnitude of caring for God's people, Solomon was so des-perate that he sacrificed one thousand burnt offerings to the Lord. It was a powerful cry for God's help, and one that God heard. That night as Solomon slept, the Lord appeared to him in a dream and said, "Ask. What should I give you?" Solomon replied to God,

> Now, O Lord my God, You have made Your servant king instead of David my father, and I am but a lad [in wisdom and experience]; I know not how to go out (begin) or come in (finish). Your servant is in the midst of Your people whom You have chosen, a great people who cannot be counted for multitude. So give Your servant an understanding mind and a hearing heart to judge Your people, that I may discern between good and bad. For who is able to judge and rule this Your great people? (1 Kings 3:7–9 AMP)

Imagine God's offering to grant a wish to you, an opportunity to ask God for anything. Solomon could have asked for riches, beauty, honor, or respect, any of the world's greatest treasures. What did he ask for? *Wisdom.* Given such an opportunity, King Solomon asked God to grant him wisdom so he could be an obedient leader of God's people. The king's response revealed his heart's desire to serve God.

God granted Solomon's request but gave him much more, something I find amazingly typical of God. Not only did God grant Solomon a wise and understanding heart, more than anyone had ever known before or after his time, but God also gave the king what he did not ask for: riches and honor, and a promise of a long life if Solomon would walk in God's ways.

Solomon requested wisdom to take care of the treasure that God had lain in his arms: God's own people, the Israelites. Like Solomon, we have also been given a great responsibility, that of caring for one (or more) of God's children. Yes, it's a daunting task, but know that God waits to give to us wisdom and understanding for our kids just as He did for King Solomon. We only have to ask for it.

God hasn't dumped this great charge into your lap and walked away. He knows very well how complicated bringing up a special needs child can be. He knows all that will be required of you in order to succeed, and He also knows that you can do it with His help. He wants to help you take care of His child. In the process, He wants you to be blessed like you have never been blessed before—divinely blessed.

Parents, consider that you stand before a mountain—a mountain that represents autism. In ascending this mountain you are caring for a child of God. God is waiting eagerly to help you reach the mountain's peak. As you stand at its base and look up, the summit is very high, much higher than any mountain around. This will be no typical ascension. Instead, it's the climb of your lifetime, because you'll be hiking along in the very presence of God.

God wants to take you to the summit of this mountain. It's going to be a sacred journey, and when you reach the top, the view from the summit is breathtaking! I want you to know that there are few tasks as sacred as caring for one of God's own.

Don't waste time! Ask God to grant you wisdom to care for your child. He promises to give it to you freely.

Promises to Treasure

For discernment

Call to Me and I will answer you and show you great and mighty things, fenced in and hidden, which you do not know (do not distinguish and recognize, have knowledge of and understand).

—Jeremiah 33:3 (amp)

For wisdom

Now if any of you lacks wisdom, he should ask God, who gives to all generously and without criticizing, and it will be given to him.

—James 1:5

Your trust justified

I couldn't stop thanking God for you—every time I prayed, I'd think of you and give thanks. But I do more than thank.

I ask—ask the God of our Master, Jesus Christ, the God of glory—to make you intelligent and discerning in knowing him personally, your eyes focused and clear, so that you can see exactly what it is he is calling you to do, grasp the immensity of this glorious way of life he has for his followers, oh, the utter extravagance of his work in us who trust him—endless energy, boundless strength!

—Ephesians 1:16–19 (msg)

God has what you need

In Him all the treasures of wisdom and knowledge are hidden.

—Colossians 2:3

Chapter 7

The Greatest Therapy

God's Promise of the Power of Love

He heals the brokenhearted and binds up their wounds.
PSALM 147:3

Alec is different.

He's a beautiful boy with an infectious smile and a rolling laugh. He has a great sense of humor. He's an awesome brother and a good son. Time and time again, people who take the time to know him fall in love with him.

But he's different than other boys. He's slower. He's not as coordinated with his motor skills. He's not the best at sports. He tries, but he can't move as fast as other boys. During his elementary school's spring and fall quarter-mile runs, he finishes last.

But I don't mind. The important thing is that Alec finishes the run. He never stops running, not even for a few steps. He keeps on going, although sometimes with his hands over his ears to protect his sensitive hearing from the cheers of parents. He gets his little blue ribbon and wears it proudly all day.

Some of the other boys in the classroom are beginning to notice that Alec, at six, can't keep up with them. Tonight, as I sit down at Alec's bedside to say our prayers, Alec has a few special prayers to say.

"God, I pray for those crazy boys in my class." Alec always mentions the "crazy boys" in his class, telling me of their "games." I never knew until tonight what those games were.

"What about those boys, Alec?" I ask.

"They laugh at me." His face shows no emotion, so I'm confused. Does he understand that they're being mean to him?

"When, Alec?" I study my son. "When do they laugh at you?"

"On recess." Alec doesn't use a lot of descriptive language, so I usually have to pry the details out of him. "They beat me."

At first I'm alarmed, not sure what he means by the word *beat*, but Alec has more to say tonight.

"They beat me when I run laps. Then they laugh at me."

I watch his face carefully, searching his eyes, looking for signs. I can't see a trace of emotion, so I'm still not sure if he's aware that his classmates are bullying him.

"Alec, when they laugh, how does that make you feel?" I gently ask him. "Are you angry?"

"Sometimes I cry."

Oh . . . so he does understand. Again, I have underestimated my son.

"Sometimes I'm angry."

I don't know what to say. I watch his precious little face. He is so handsome, so beautiful. He is such a gift to our family, and I am so very blessed to be his mama.

"Alec," I whisper as I cup my hands to his soft cheeks and turn them to me. "Alec. I think you are wonderful."

Then Alec says something to me, and his words sink deep into my soul, never to be forgotten. Something that shows me he's well aware of the bullying and feels the sting of it. Something that tells me he's been hiding his pain.

"Thanks for telling me that," he says to me, as if he's been desperate for affirmation.

My eyes fill up with tears, but there's nothing I can do but kiss him and whisper, "Good night, Alec. Sleep well."

The Father of a "Different" Son

Let me tell you about a father whose son was also . . . well . . . "different."

When the boy was born he seemed normal enough. His mother welcomed him into her arms. She sang lullabies to him and watched her firstborn as he slept. She wrapped him tightly to keep him warm and no doubt dreamed of a bright and purposeful future for her little lad, a future of promise and hope. She treasured such dreams in her heart, pulling them out from time to time, surely wondering about the great purpose her child would certainly find.

The little boy was welcomed into the world with gifts, some extravagant and some small. People came to visit the family, bringing greetings and well wishes. As the child grew, his family moved from time to time, taking their young son with them. They were a faith-filled family, though not rich or especially notable in society, and like most mothers, his would have done everything she could to provide a home full of love for this boy. His father made sure he was protected and cared for in every way.

It became apparent in his preteen years that this little man, while not autistic, was unlike the other children. For example, he had an intense obsession for heavenly things, preferring to spend his time studying anything and everything related to God. With each passing year, it became more noticeable that something set him apart from others. Even so, he was a prince in his father's eyes, who did not hesitate to let the world know that this child was his own treasured son. He was very pleased with his boy.

Years went by and the boy grew to be a man. To others, he seemed to live his life his own way, forging new paths instead of taking the more popular routes. In doing so, he found that most people didn't understand him at all. At times others blatantly mocked him, and some were downright hateful. Most didn't tolerate that he wasn't like them—not "one of the guys"—so they insulted him in various ways. Maybe he intimidated them in some way by his peculiar manner, or maybe they simply didn't take the time to get to know him. Perhaps they were afraid of what others might think if they befriended him.

The son became a wanderer. He didn't settle down in any one place to pursue a career, but instead traveled from town to town, living out a unique purpose that no one—not even the closest of his few friends or family—fully understood.

And his father saw it all: the taunts of others, the disgusted glares, the whispers as his son passed them on the street. But, oh, how he loved his boy! He believed in him always, standing by him even when the loyalty of his son's few close friends wavered.

The father saw goodness in the young man that the world failed to see. He saw the compassion his son showed to people whom everyone else shunned. He saw a man who stood up for the underdog, the poor and unloved in life. He saw someone who took the time to speak with those to whom others wouldn't give the time of day. Yes, the father knew that his son would even go so far as to give his own life for another, asking for nothing in return. His son was an amazing man, and he made sure his son knew how he felt, saying to him "You are my son, whom I love; with you I am well pleased."

That love strengthened the son, helping him endure some really demanding days. He knew his father loved him, and with this knowledge he was able to withstand the taunting of others. He never forgot that he was his father's beloved son, and knowing this was enough to carry him through his darkest day and on to a purpose greater than anyone could begin to comprehend.

On a day so black and dark that the ground shook, the son was cruelly murdered—betrayed by a "friend." Eventually, in giving so much of himself, he lost everything. His few other friends turned their backs on him that day, but he chose to keep loving them anyway.

The incredible love of the father empowered the son to face each and every rejection with grace. Incredibly, the son returned love for hatred, and mercy for injustice. In doing so, he was able to touch people's calloused hearts in miraculous ways.

The world took everything from this man, including his life, but he left a wake of love that continues on and on, changing lives generation after generation. Through him, people experience a love like never before, one that knows no ending. The world has never been the same.

In case you haven't guessed by now, this Son was Jesus, the One who gave His life to bring us back to the Father.

Parents, I want you to know that your heavenly Father understands what it feels like to be the parent of a child the world just doesn't get. The Father understands more than we could ever know. That's why I know deep in my spirit that God's very heart is for children with autism. You see, He's been there with us.

A God Who Understands Us

Parents always suffer when their children suffer. Sometimes it seems that the world turns its back on our precious, unique, and God-designed kids. Other kids tease or torment our autistic child for being "different." (I prefer to describe our kids as unique, as we are all individuals, special in our own way.) Parents don't invite our children to neighborhood birthday parties or sleepovers. Sometimes rejection comes from places where we wouldn't expect to find it, such as in Sunday school or in the public classrooms and private schools.

It breaks our hearts, because we know how much our little ones have to give. We so want the world to see our child as we do. Our kids want to be understood and welcomed, even if delays in social development prevent them from reaching out in acceptable ways. We lament, "If only others knew my child as I do!"

It's important to know that God understands our pain and frustrations as we watch the world react unkindly to our precious kids. He has a great empathy for our sorrows because, as the father of Jesus, He watched His own son suffer taunts, jeers, and loneliness. He watched from heaven as the world took the great love of Jesus, like a beautiful rose, and trampled it. Jesus was sent to give a priceless gift to the world, but we did not understand Him. Instead, we ran from Him. We hid from Him—we still do even today. And God sees it all.

God knows the heart of a parent. That's why it's imperative that we go to God with these hurts, because He's been there. Psalm 34:15 promises us this: "The eyes of the LORD are on the righteous, and His ears are open to their cry for help."

Warren W. Wiersbe explains the promise of Psalm 34:15 in this way: "The assurance is that God is near us when our hearts and spirits are crushed, whether we feel like [He is] or not. This is not a promise with conditions attached to it; *it is a fact*."[1]

We cannot always be there to wrap our arms around our child and shield him or her from the world. We can't be there when a classmate calls her an ugly name, or when no one will play with him. But rest assured, God is there with our babies, at all times and in all places. This is a source of reassurance to me each morning as I watch Alec run into school with his SpongeBob backpack smiling back at me. He may be out of my arms, but he's never out of God's hand.

The Power of Love to Overcome Autism

One of the most underestimated forces in this world is love. With a simple touch, it can break down walls. It seeps deep into our souls and has a life-giving quality about it. Like water to a desert-parched traveler, it restores. Without it, we wither. Love changes us. It has an ability to open our eyes to see a person or child as God does: beautiful and divinely created. Love enables us to go just a little farther, to give just a little more, even when we feel that we've reached the very end of our rope. Love multiplies itself, having a strange quality of never running out. The more it is given, the more it returns to us.

One of love's many mysteries is that as we empty ourselves of "self," we create a place for God's love to abide. As we give to others, we are given more; as we love others, we become more aware of the Father's great love for us. It's as if we are a great channel, an open vessel, for God's love to flow through. We are His arms, His hands, and His feet. When we chose to love, His divine presence fills our lives with joy, peace, and a sense of purpose. We are, at last, fulfilled.

Love bolsters our children, enabling them to keep on going. Love encourages, supports, and strengthens. Love chooses to look past the frail and confused exterior and see the full potential of a child, the potential to be more and do more than the world expects. Love verifies the worth of each child when the world demeans him or her. It carries our children when they cannot carry themselves.

When we love a child who has autism, something profound happens to us. I see the truth of this statement again and again as I get to know other parents of autistic kids. These parents are some of the most radiant beings on this earth. Even struggling with all of the responsibilities they face, they have a beauty and a strength about them. There is a sincerity in their smile. They are as strong as the young warrior

David. I know of many parents who have risen above autism. No one can tell them they can't make a difference for their child. They will not take *no* for an answer when reaching out for help for their child. They take the worst that the world can give and in the process leave it a better place—all because they are continually being strengthened by the giving and receiving of love via a child with autism.

I know that I've been changed for the better in knowing Alec. Never before did I have a passion for children as I do now. Prior to this journey, the biggest dream I possessed was simply to be a star employee in the marketing department where I worked. Never did I have a dream of making a difference for others or of encouraging another to be more, do more, or live in a better way. Before Alec, the dream of writing a book was so unrealistic, I stuffed it deep inside. It was too dangerous to believe. Yet, in walking with Alec, I can risk even the most risky of God-given dreams.

Loving Alec has changed me forever. The things I once valued so highly seem so insignificant to me now. I've learned to live for better things—to help my children fulfill their potential and to help other parents do the same for their children. I now know the indescribable joy in loving someone so much that my heart feels as if it will burst.

This love spills out around me like water from a fountain, going its own way, reaching out to others. Invariably, the power of that love touches and changes others. Love multiplies as we pay it forward, and repeatedly I see the proof that it returns to us.

When you love a child who has autism, you're giving something sacred to that child. That love has a power, an essence. The divine touch of God exists within this love: "We know it so well, we've embraced it heart and soul, this love that comes from God. God is love. When we take up permanent residence in a life of love, we live in God and God lives in us" (1 John 4:16–17 MSG).

Knowing that the very presence of God's love dwells within us, how can we put a limit on what it can do for our child—or for us? How dare we think that He is incapable of helping us in our battle with autism?

I'm convinced that God can do far more than we dare to dream.

PROMISES TO TREASURE

Eternal love

"Though the mountains move and the hills shake, My love will not be removed from you and My covenant of peace will not be shaken," says your compassionate LORD.

—ISAIAH 54:10

God's love has no beginning

Long before he laid down earth's foundations, he had us in mind, had settled on us as the focus of his love, to be made whole and holy by his love. Long, long ago he decided to adopt us into his family through Jesus Christ. (What pleasure he took in planning this!) He wanted us to enter into the celebration of his lavish gift-giving by the hand of his beloved Son.

—EPHESIANS 1:4–6 (MSG)

God's love has no end

I'm absolutely convinced that nothing—nothing living or dead, angelic or demonic, today or tomorrow, high or low, thinkable or unthinkable—absolutely nothing can get between us and God's love because of the way that Jesus our Master has embraced us.

—ROMANS 8:38–39 (MSG)

God's love dwells in us

And hope does not disappoint us, because God has poured out his love into our hearts by the Holy Spirit, whom he has given us.

—ROMANS 5:5 (NIV)

The depth of God's love is infinite

This is how God showed his love for us: God sent his only Son into the world so we might live through him. This is the kind of love we are talking about—not that we once upon a time loved God, but that he loved us and sent his Son as a sacrifice to clear away our sins and the damage they've done to our relationship with God.

—1 JOHN 4:9–10 (MSG)

Chapter 8

When Depression Comes Knocking

God's Promise of Hope

Thus says the Lord: Restrain your voice from weeping and your eyes from tears, for your work shall be rewarded, says the Lord; and [your children] shall return from the enemy's land. And there is hope for your future, says the Lord; your children shall come back to their own country.

JEREMIAH 31:16–17 (AMP)

Shortly after I learned that Alec was autistic, I sat across from two sweet ladies in a secluded prayer room at our church. I held onto their hands tightly as we spoke in hushed tones. These women, gently touching my shoulders as if to bear me up, whispered prayers of hope and love with me, a frightened, confused, and despondent mother whom they'd never met before. In their early sixties, they held an outward appearance of soft-spoken Southern women, but I know this was only their facade. Behind those sweet exteriors, those ladies were clothed in God's armor. Members of God's army of intercessory prayer warriors, these women stood with me before the throne. They whispered bold prayers as I struggled to hold my composure.

After spilling out the contents of my heart to these ladies, telling them about my fears, my selfish thoughts, and ensuing depression, they didn't toss me a platitude by saying, "I'll pray for you." Instead, these ladies hugged me and shared my tears. Only after allowing me to reveal the contents of my heart did they begin to pray. During that prayer, one of these women gave me a promise of hope that I hold on to even today: she told me that my son would be healed, but that it would take a long time.

You can say what you will, but I've held on to that promise. I can't justify it to you. I only know that I took those words and engraved them on my soul. I speak that promise audibly in my nightly prayers over Alec, asking God that my son will be "all the man that God intended him to be." This is my prayer for Alec, that God's plan for him will be fulfilled. Maybe that is the healing the prayer warrior prophesied, but I think it's more. Like I said, I can't justify it to you or anyone else. I can only hold on to that hope with every ounce of my being. I promise you this: I will not let it go.

Even today, I hope for Alec's healing. Not a partial healing, but a complete and total healing. My heart's desire is to sit down with my son and engage in deep, thoughtful conversations about God and His magnificent creation. And yet I love the boy just as he is—every remarkable, beautiful bit of him. He's one of the most precious gifts I've ever received from God.

Some people say that if I pray for his healing, I must not truly love my son just as he is. They question how I can desire that my son live without autism, and at the same time be content with him as he is today. Yet these people can't know my heart and how it overflows with love for that boy.

I can rejoice today because I know life is a journey, a process. The goal is always in sight, but it's the getting there that is glorious. I will continue to press on, striving for all that God has for me and for my son.

When Depression Hits

My father, who has suffered enough loss to fill the pages of his own book, taught me the difference between grief and depression. The difference is this: when a person is grieving a loss, they still have a hope for the future. With depression, however, there is an absence of hope. God does not want us to live without hope!

So what do you do when you've reached the pit and hope has faded away? Where do you go when each day brings seemingly insurmountable frustrations and you've reached the end of your resources? What do you do when you've tried every therapy out there, spending all that you have, and nothing has made your child any better? What do you do when you feel powerless to help your child?

If this is where you are today, you'll find encouragement in God's Word: "So let us seize and hold fast and retain without wavering the hope we cherish and confess and our acknowledgement of it, for He Who promised is reliable (sure) and faithful to His word" (Heb. 10:23 AMP).

Child of God, you are not alone! Your hope is grounded not in your own abilities—but in God's love, power, and faithfulness! When life is so difficult that we can't even turn our gaze to the heavens, God comes to our rescue as the "lifter of our head" (Ps. 3:3 AMP). He gently cups our chin and directs our eyes to Him.

Parents, know that God is not finished working in your life just yet! Your story is not complete. Wait for Him, because the tide of hope will come in again, lifting us up and over despair.

If you're depressed, without hope, God provides a balm for this depression in His Word. In order for it to work, though, you must read His Word, rubbing the ointment of His promises of hope into your very soul.

Here's one way to do that: purchase a journal and as you read Scripture and discover one of God's promises, write it down. When you do, ask God to honor that promise for you and your child. Record the date of your request and keep on breathing. Keep on walking. As God honors a promise, record it in your journal. Keeping track of requests and their being honored is important because, in time, you'll find each page filled with dates scribbled in your journal's margins alongside of the promises, a visual proof that God is there with you both in the past and right now. This may seem like a small thing, but as your faith grows from seeing God work in your life, your hope in the Lord will also grow. When hope walks in the room, depression walks out.

Although you may not understand what God is doing in your life, know that He does have a plan. It's hard not to worry about the future, but God promises His children a "future and a hope":

> "For I know the plans I have for you," declares the LORD, "plans to prosper you and not to harm you, plans to give you hope and a future. Then you will call upon me and come and pray to me, and I will listen to you. You will seek me and find me when you seek me with all your heart. I will be found by you," declares the LORD, "and will bring you back from captivity." (Jer. 29:11–14 NIV)

The Importance of Community: Shared Hope

Let me tell you a secret: I'm an introvert. I break out in a sweat when I find myself in a room of strangers. I have great difficulty starting up a conversation with a person I've just met. I'm not outgoing, except for a few short years in college when I became a social butterfly. But then, college does strange things to the human psyche, doesn't it?

My husband, Matt, however, is an extrovert, and conversation comes easily to him. He has the gift of the spoken word, like his mother and sister, and loves to meet new people to swap stories with them. I wish I could be more like the Langston clan socially, but I'm more of a Charlie Brown in social situations. When, for example, I'm at a meeting and the icebreakers begin, I suddenly feel the urge to take a bathroom break. But alas, sometimes the exits are blocked and I can't dodge these dreaded exercises. Forced to comply, I turn to the closest friendly face and typically say something . . . anything. Usually it's really dumb. Then I spend the next ten minutes ignoring the program while I mentally rework the conversation until I sound more like Maya Angelo than Homer Simpson.

I've always preferred to carry my own load, choosing to say, "no thanks, I'm fine," whenever anyone offers help. When I do need help, I typically won't ask for it, so as not to burden anyone else. I'd rather struggle along all by myself. Like I said, I'm an introvert, but God is working on me. Alec has even helped me in this area. When I learned that my son had autism, I had to get over my fear of talking to strangers, and without delay.

To all my fellow introverted parents out there, please understand that autism is a series of hurdles in your life, and you need a boost to clear them. That boost needs to come from someone other than you. Because the variations in symptoms are so extreme and so little is known about autism spectrum disorders, parents must reach out for support from others. God has provided a wonderful community of help out there, and they know a lot about the size, shape, and number of hurdles in your path.

My family wouldn't be where we are today on our journey if it weren't for the help of parents who are farther down a similar road. Time and time again, I've found parents of children with autism spectrum disorders to be more than willing to share their stories and insights. The state chapters of the Autism Society of America can tell you where to meet other parents. If you're in a rural area or unable to find other parents locally, or if you want to meet other parents via the Web, many online discussion and e-mail groups are available to plug you into the vast network of shared parental expertise. (See appendix B.)

No one understands the difficulties of raising a child with autism better than another parent of an ASD child. They understand what you're going through, and most are more than willing to share their knowledge with you. They'll tell you the good experiences they've had, and they'll warn you of the pitfalls they've encountered.

The bottom line is, don't choose to walk alone. Other parents have blazed trails to make your walk easier. You have to reach out to find them, but don't be afraid to ask for support. It's not hard to find it.

Having a group of parents from whom to glean advice and recommendations is so valuable. But, by all means, do your own research in order to make the best decisions you can in terms of providers. You know your child best. Then pass on to others what you've learned.

Finding a Reason to Keep Going

When Alec was four, he attended Garr Christian Academy's preschool, a local private school that provides an excellent curriculum for children with autism. Each afternoon during that year, I pulled my car into the parking lot a few minutes early, waiting for the teachers to walk the children out to meet their parents. There I'd sit in the car line, waiting for my son.

Day after day, I watched those kids as their mothers and fathers enthusiastically jumped out of the car to greet them after their long hours of hard work. Sitting in my car, I studied the children's reactions as they were ushered to their parents. For a neurotypical child, the arrival of mom and dad causes great excitement. The children rush into their parent's arms, cheering "Mommy!" or "Daddy!" with arms open wide for the "Big Pick-up."

But things were different at Alec's school. Strangely, it was the parents who ran to their children, arms extended for a reverse version of the "Big Pick-up." Children with autism and sensory integration disorders often find hugs and excitement alarming. Consequently, as the kids were lifted into the air by a parent, I didn't see the ear-to-ear grins that I saw on neurotypical children when picking up my daughter at her school.

At first, this bothered me. I was saddened to see the apparent disconnect between parent and child. This should be one of the best parts of a child's day! But as the days went by and I watched more closely, I looked deeper, studying the children's eyes as they were lifted into their parent's arms.

Then it happened. I saw something there that I hadn't noticed before, a glint of light, a flicker, a flash of glee, something that sparkled tenderly in their eyes if only for a brief but glorious moment. Seeing this, I was overwhelmed with joy. I was given the gift of understanding a secret language, expressed deep within the children's eyes when their mamas and papas lifted them into the air. Yes, the excitement and joy were there after all. I watched more closely, and each day I could see the sparkle in their eyes as their parents greeted them.

In that tiny shimmer of recognition and love, I saw hope. I understood that, in order to reach Alec, I must learn to "speak" his uncommon language. He was there waiting for me, waiting to receive all the love that I had, and to give it back to me, but I had some work to do. Our children with autism are entirely capable of receiving and giving love, but we need to speak their language.

Hope has always been there. God places the seeds of it deep within our hearts. As we reach out to understand our children with love and compassion, the seed is watered and grows.

Hoping for the Impossible: Asking for God's Healing Touch

If the sacrifice of Christ gives us the authority to ask God for anything, surely that doesn't really mean *anything*, does it? Can parents pray for something that is realistically impossible yet with the hope that God will grant our request? Can we ask for the healing of our children? If we do muster enough courage to ask, what happens if we harbor a secret doubt in God's ability to heal our child? Does this nullify our prayer? What if there is sin in our lives? Will that prevent our children from receiving God's healing touch?

First things first: Yes, we can ask God for *anything*. We can ask God for the healing of our children. As Jesus prepared the disciples for His departure from this world by way of the cross, He comforted them with these words:

> Believe me when I say that I am in the Father and the Father is in me; or at least believe on the evidence of the miracles themselves. I tell you the truth, anyone who has faith in me will do what I have been doing. He will do even greater things than these, because I am going to the Father. And I will do whatever you ask in my name, so that the Son may bring glory to the Father. You may ask me for anything in my name, and I will do it. (John 14:11–14 NIV)

What was it that Jesus had been doing? The Gospels tell us that Jesus had, by healing the sick and handicapped, provided evidence that God was, indeed, within Him. Multitudes thronged around Jesus for this very reason, and His compassion for the suffering was striking. In the above verses, Jesus stresses that His words are the truth: we can ask God for anything in His name, including healing.

But wait a minute. Many of us know people who've valiantly fought a terminal disease. We've listened to their distressed prayers for healing, and we've been shaken when they died without receiving it. How, then, can we ask for such a thing without doubt, when we see countless prayers for healing that rise to the heavens and seem to be ignored? My own father wrestled with this question at a time when grief and despair seemed to be his closest friends.

My father, Ted Smith Jr., is a retired steel worker, a Christian man who has walked with God for much of his life. During his thirty-plus years of employment at a now-demolished coke-processing plant in southern Ohio, Dad shared the gospel with his fellow workers. Although covered head-to-toe with the coal black soot of the coke-producing ovens, Dad was illuminated by the love of Christ, a light that intensified over the years as he shared the life of Jesus with his coworkers. Working in an economically depressed region of southern Ohio, Dad served as the mill's unofficial pastor, an evangelist without a seminary degree. In serving the men at the mill, Dad found a holy purpose and joy in a terribly depressing environment.

During those years Dad had one fervent prayer of his own. While she was still in her twenties, Dad's beautiful wife Vickie, my stepmother, was diagnosed with multiple sclerosis. My father began to pray for Vickie's healing. As the years rolled by, Dad's prayers became more frequent and increasingly fervent. Even so, Vickie's health continued to decline. It seemed to me as if God did not hear my father's most urgent prayer. Was God ignoring my Dad, a man who lived to testify about God's love, and who helped shoulder so many burdens not his own? Where was God, anyway? Why wasn't He answering?

Despite trips to specialists and participation in promising drug trials, Vickie eventually lost the ability to walk. Determined to keep his wife in her own home, Dad bought a medical bed and lovingly tended to her with the help of nursing care. Life was arduous in those years, but my father and Vickie never lost their ability to laugh a little each day, holding fast to a God-given sense of humor that carried them through many wearisome nights. Night after night and year after year, Dad incessantly prayed that God would heal his beloved wife.

"I never, not for one instant, doubted that God had the ability to heal Vickie," Dad recalls. "Often well-intentioned people would tell me that if only I had enough faith, God would heal her." That advice served only to anger my father. He was certain of God's *ability* to heal his wife. He just didn't know if healing was a part of God's plan for Vickie's life with him.

Finally in 2001, God called Vickie home. My father did not witness the miracle of her healing, a request for which he had been pleading for nearly twenty years. Grieving, and alone for the first time in decades, my father's faith took a severe blow. He found himself in a sea of despair, struggling to keep his head above the waves. Grasping for a lifeline of hope, Dad began to doubt God. Nonetheless, my father had walked with God for many years, and he knew that God was big enough to handle his doubts. Dad decided to gather them up and take them straight to Jesus.

My father's walk with Jesus is not only spiritual, but also physical. He takes long hikes in the mornings, watching the sunlight filter through the tree canopy while silently conversing with God, as if discussing life with a good friend. Having suffered the loss of his wife and best friend, Dad needed to know something. He needed to know if he was merely wasting his time believing in more than what he could see and touch. So one morning during his daily walk, he poured out his heart, asking, "God, are You for real?" In his state of grief, my father held nothing back. Walking in the quiet, he silently fumed, "Is all of this faith business of Yours true, or is it just some namby-pamby story we create?"

Sometime during his walk, the Holy Spirit, whom Jesus called the "Comforter" (see John 14:16 AMP), reminded my father of the story of John the Baptist, about whom Jesus Himself declared, "Truly I tell you, among those born of women there has not risen anyone greater than John the Baptist" (Matt. 11:11 AMP). John had been imprisoned for many months and was under great physical and emotional strain. After receiving reports of Jesus' miraculous healings throughout Judea,

John, stressed and suffering from uncertainty, took his doubt straight to the Savior. He sent two of his disciples and instructed them to ask of Jesus, "Are You the One who is to come, or should we look for someone else?" (Luke 7:19).

Jesus' response to John was full of compassion. "Go and report to John the things you have seen and heard: The blind receive their sight, the lame walk, those with skin diseases are healed, the deaf hear, the dead are raised, and the poor have the good news preached to them" (Luke 7:22). In other words, Jesus was saying, "Yes, John! I am He! Look no further!"

It's so comforting to know that God can take on our doubt, and that we never need to be afraid to take our darkest thoughts to Jesus. Dad laid bare his confused and questioning soul during a typical morning stroll. While in prayer, Dad was reminded that even the greatest of spiritual leaders can doubt during times of calamity. My father was no different; he was human.

Amazingly, God had another message for Dad the next day. While he stood in Vickie's room—where she had been bedridden for so many years, unable to chase her favorite cat or jump up to hug her precious grandchildren—his senses were suddenly washed by a presence in the room, like an invisible wave of familiarity. Instantly he knew that Vickie was alive in soul and spirit. Dad saw no vision, but to his joy, he immediately understood that God had answered his prayer after all. Overcome with a sudden peace and joy, Dad realized that, in heaven, Vickie was, at last, well.

That day was a turning point for my father. After that miraculous moment, Dad started living life again. Dad saw that his prayer had been answered, although not in the way he'd wished.

We, too, need to remember that there is more to life than what we see and experience here on earth. God has much more in store for us and our children. The truth is that our prayers are always answered. Sometimes the answer is "yes," and sometimes it's "no." At other times, it's simply "not yet," but rest assured, every prayer will be answered, so ask and do not doubt. Remember, dear parents, our prayers for healing are never wasted. We can hold fast to our hope, knowing for certain that God hears us and answers when we call.

Alec's Hope of Healing

An adversary always lurks nearby, and he tells me there's no hope that my son will ever leave autism behind. I refuse to believe it. This is the hope I will never relinquish: I hope for my son the fulfillment of every single promise that is revealed in God's Word. I know that God will honor every single one of His promises, including the promise of healing: "'But I will restore you to health and heal your wounds,' declares the Lord, 'because you are called an outcast, Zion for whom no one cares'" (Jer. 30:17 niv).

I hold fast to the hope that my son will be all that God intended him to be on this earth, and that His plan for Alec, special and divine in purpose, will be fulfilled in this lifetime. My friends, Alec may walk every day of his earthly life battling autism. No doctor may ever say that he has been healed of the disorder. Perhaps my son will require interventions and therapies for the rest of his life.

But I can promise you this: one day, my sweet son will close his eyes to this world for the last time. If on that day his hospital chart still contains the word "autism," then this I know beyond a shadow of doubt: in the next split second Jesus will awaken Alec to a new and better life, and one that will never end. When my precious son's eyes take in the glory of that world, I know that autism will be a distant memory.

In the brilliant glory of God's eternity, there will be no trace—not the slightest breath—of autism. On that day, Alec will be healed, and not just partially—completely and forever healed.

Oh, yes, I'm holding fast for that day!

· ·

Promises to Treasure

God created your child for His glory

So don't be afraid: I'm with you. I'll round up all your scattered children, pull them in from east and west. I'll send orders north and south: "Send them back. Return my sons from distant lands, my daughters from faraway places. I want them back, every last one who bears my name, every man, woman,

and child whom I created for my glory, yes, personally formed
and made each one."

—Isaiah 43:5–7 (msg)

God sustains life

I will never forget your precepts,
for by them you have preserved my life.

—Psalm 119:93 (niv)

Healing

But for you who fear My name, the sun of righteousness will
rise with healing in its wings, and you will go out and playfully
jump like calves from the stall.

—Malachi 4:2

Joy aids in healing

A joyful heart is good medicine,
but a broken spirit dries up the bones.

—Proverbs 17:22

Jesus can heal

Just then, a woman who had suffered from bleeding for 12
years approached from behind and touched the tassel on His
robe, for she said to herself, "If I can just touch His robe, I'll
be made well!" But Jesus turned and saw her. "Have courage,
daughter," He said. "Your faith has made you well." And the
woman was made well from that moment.

—Matthew 9:20–22

Chapter 9

When the Bully Taunts

God's Promise of Our Incredible Worth

And the LORD *has declared this day that you are his people,*
his treasured possession as he promised, and that you are to
keep all his commands. He has declared that he will set you
in praise, fame and honor high above all the nations he has
made and that you will be a people holy to the LORD *your*
God, as he promised.

DEUTERONOMY 26:18–19 (NIV)

Sticks and stones may break my bones, but words will never hurt me.

These words rumble in our own heads like distant thunder when a bully targets our child. Often as attempts to elevate their own fragile sense of self-worth, bullies attack children considered vulnerable or "different." Whenever they stumble across an opportunity, bullies have a pocketful of hurtful names to launch as ammunition. Children with autism often come into contact with bullies at schools or in their neighborhoods.

When our children, hurt written all over their faces, tell us of their run-ins with bullies, we know the old cliché is incorrect. The barrage of ugly words does cause emotional pain. What can we do to protect our children's sense of self-worth after the attack of an insult slinger?

Worth That Rests in the Wrong Place

"Earthquake!"

I'm eleven years old, running through the parking lot of my mother's

apartment complex when I pass them. The group of four boys are lean-
ing against a chain-link fence. *Don't look at them*, I tell myself, flushed
from the exertion of my plump body, and now from embarrassment.
Keep running, just keep running. With eyes fixed on some imaginary
object ahead of me, I jog by the boys, determined to press on.

I was in sixth grade, a girl with few friends and a lot of excess
weight. This was me, the target of neighborhood and school bullies, in
the years following the divorce of my parents. Only a few years earlier
I'd stood on the round, cabled rug in the middle of my bedroom with
my mother kneeling in front of me. With her face to mine, she told
me that my daddy would not be coming home again. I was eight at
the time, an introverted second-grader, and I believed that I must have
done something wrong to cause my father to go. A feeling of useless-
ness filled me as I watched my mother cry, wanting to comfort her but
not knowing how.

My parents loved me very much and never meant to cause me any
pain. They were two people who were hurting, trying to fix a marriage
but without the tools necessary to do so. At eight years of age, I could
do nothing but watch my world crumble around me, caught in the debris of a broken marriage.

During those years I came home from school and headed straight
for the refrigerator. I'd grab some candy and chips, or marshmallow
cream and handfuls of cereal, and turn on the television. I'd sit there
for hours, stuffing my pain with Cheetos, cupcakes, and candy bars. By
the time I was in fifth grade, I'd gained so much weight that my pediatrician warned my mother that I would weigh two hundred pounds by
high school if I kept binging my pain away. My parents tried to help me
by offering diet suggestions, but I wasn't listening.

Food was a comfort to me, but it was only a Band-Aid for the hurt I
felt inside. During fourth and fifth grade, I was beyond what I'd term
as "chubby," which was no condition for winning friends in a new elementary school. Soon enough, kids began to call me some pretty vi-
cious names. I walked home many days during fourth and fifth grade
with my arms full of books and my long brown hair sticking to the
tears on my cheeks.

Day after day, my mother wiped tears away from my eyes and whispered to me, "Kelly, you're such a beautiful girl. God has a special plan for you, I just know it." Turning my face to hers, she promised, "Just wait, you'll see, and so will everyone else."

In the sixth grade, my father encouraged me to take up jogging. I was eating a McDonald's apple pie at the time, sitting on the sofa watching television as he stood before me, telling me he could feel my pain. I was always eager to please him, so I said I'd give it a try. When I started, I could run only two blocks, huffing and puffing my way past each house on the way. It wasn't far, but Dad made a big fuss over me, and I did feel a sense of pride whenever I ran.

"Do you see the people in the passing cars looking at you?" He puffed as we ran down the boulevard of my small town. "They wish that they could do this, too!" I kept his encouragements and locked the words safely inside my heart, ready to be pulled out whenever a neighborhood bully offered his own street-side commentary of my run.

In time, I was able to run a little farther, enjoying the postrun euphoria and the feeling that I was capable of more than sitting and eating. With each mile and each step, my self-esteem grew and my excess weight began to melt. After a while, I didn't mind the nasty taunts of the neighborhood bullies as I ran by. Eventually they lost interest in me. By the time I returned to school in the seventh grade, I was a brand-new girl with a renewed sense of self-worth and a strength that I never knew I possessed.

My sense of self-worth was fragile, however, for it depended on the approval of others. I wanted so much to be loved, and deep inside I felt I could be loved only if I met the expectations of others. As long as the scale was kind to me and I was surrounded by friends, I was happy. My sense of worth was reactive rather than proactive. The amount of joy in my life was controlled by how far the needle traveled on my bathroom scale.

This was the way I lived for years, my worth dependent on external factors and as fragile as rice paper. That is, until I discovered my true worth in God's eyes.

The Hardest Truth to Believe

I'm no different than you. We've all had bullies in our past—our critics—who were more than happy to sprinkle a little negativity on our day. Everyone has a story or two about a friend, relative, or acquaintance who trampled all over his or her fragile ego with soul-crushing, steel-toed boots. And do you know what? If we're honest, we've probably worn those boots ourselves a time or two, shamelessly stomping on someone else with our own unwarranted verbal jabs.

That's why it's critically important for parents to know what God says about our worth if we're to teach our little one the truth of who he or she really is: God's much-loved child. Society is always ready to tell us that we're less than who we really are; that we're used, defective; not attractive enough, wealthy enough, or smart enough; too old, too fat, utterly worthless.

God tells us another story, and it's the real one: we are priceless and infinitely valued. Here's the proof: God withheld nothing to bring us back to Him, not even His own Son (John 3:16). The truth is that we do have a purpose (Prov. 19:21), and we have a divinely designed future (Jer. 31:17). We have been gifted with access to the throne of God, through Christ (Heb. 4:16), and the promise of eternity as children of the everlasting King (John 14:2).

For some reason, we tend to believe the world's lies instead of God's truth about who we are. It's hard to wrap our minds around such fantastic truths. We're conditioned by life to believe that if something sounds too good to be true, it probably is. Yet although God's promises surpass our wildest dreams, they are true! God's truth survives the test of time because a holy God—who, again, cannot lie—gives them to us.

We need to know the truth of who we really are, especially when our child comes to us, eyes stinging with tears over the ugly lies of a bully. Don't wait for a run-in with a bully to occur before you teach your child how much God values him or her; start today! Study the countless passages of that tell us just how precious we are to God, memorize the verses, accepting His words of love for your own life, and live them out so our kids see firsthand what it means to walk in the knowledge of our true worth.[1] Our true worth is found in Christ, who gave everything

He had to ransom us back to our heavenly home. God spared nothing to save us, and in that we find evidence of our immense value to our heavenly Father.

When a bully attacks our children, our children have a choice to make: they can believe what the bully says about them—the lie—or choose to believe what God says about them—the truth. Here is the difference:

THE BULLY: You're stupid. You're ugly. No one likes you. You don't belong here. You have no talent. You have nothing to offer. No one wants to listen to you. You're holding us back. Why don't you just go away? No one would notice if you did.

GOD: Don't be afraid, I've redeemed you. I've called your name. You're mine. When you're in over your head, I'll be there with you. When you're in rough waters, you will not go down. When you're between a rock and a hard place, it won't be a dead end—Because I am God, your personal God, The Holy of Israel, your Savior. I paid a huge price for you: all of Egypt, with rich Cush and Seba thrown in! That's how much you mean to me! That's how much I love you! I'd sell off the whole world to get you back, trade the creation just for you. So don't be afraid: I'm with you. (Isa. 43:1–5 MSG)

Isaiah 43:1–5 is just one of many words of love in Scripture that tell us who we really are: God's privileged heirs. But somehow one ugly word or action can cause us to lose sight of it all. Refuse to let that happen! Hold fast to the truth, our lifeline, and do not accept the deceptions of life's bullies. By reading Scripture and learning who our children really are, we can help them find their confidence in God, not man. When that happens, their lives change, and it's not a subtle change. It's dramatic! They'll find their strength in Him.

To live the life God wants us to live as Christians, we need to know that God really does love and value us. Once we understand and accept that truth, the natural by-product is a love within us that returns to God, in gratitude and in joy, and also flows out to others. "We love because He first loved us" (1 John 4:19).

If you know the fullness of God's love, then the hateful words of the bully fall flat. When our children know the truth, they will stand up to the bully with dignity.

What a Difference Thirty Years Makes

When Alec told me that some of the boys in his class were teasing him, the pain I felt was exactly the same as when those kids yelled, "Earthquake!" as I ran down the street. It was like tearing off a thirty-year-old Band-Aid and finding the wound still fresh. As I touched my own cheeks to find them hot, just like they were when the bullies teased and tormented me, I understood exactly how my son felt.

Suddenly I was thankful for the experience of being teased myself, because it enabled me to be empathetic to my son. Thirty years later, God turned my hurtful experience into a blessing. I understood Alec's pain because I had been there, too. I instinctively knew the right words to say to him, words similar to those my own mother whispered to me each day as she wiped away my own tears: "Alec, you're such a wonderful boy. God has a special plan for you, I just know it. Just wait, you'll see, and so will everyone else."

Miraculously, God turned a cruel situation into something useful, just as He promises in His Word: "You planned evil against me; God planned it for good to bring about the present result" (Gen. 50:20).

When it comes to my children I'm a big mama bear. When someone hurts my baby, my natural and immediate impulse is to strike back. Make no mistake, I'm angry at the little ones who tease my child! I can imagine a thousand embarrassing situations that I could wish for them. But I've learned from experience to pray instead, because it is infinitely better to allow God to work in the situation than to seek my own revenge.

I want to call attention to one of Satan's best traps: retaliation. If we choose to retaliate, we choose to handle the situation ourselves rather than allowing God to manage the situation by using His resources instead of our own. We choose to use our limited knowledge and power instead of the unlimited power, foresight, and omniscience of God.

We've also given Satan a stronghold and a place in our hearts to plant seeds of his favorite weed—bitterness. That's why God warns us, "Be angry and do not sin. Don't let the sun go down on your anger, and don't give the Devil an opportunity" (Eph. 4:26–27). I don't want an act of revenge or spite on my part to dam up God's flow of spirit and power in our family. Our enemy would love for me to add fuel to the fire of conflict, and so I pray for strength to do the right thing when Alec is teased. I admit, the right thing is hard to do, but that's why it takes God's help to do it.

Spurgeon urges us to look beyond our enemies to the great hope we find as children of God:

> Our enemy may put out our light for a season. There is sure hope for us in the Lord; and if we are trusting in Him and holding fast our integrity, our season of downcasting and darkness will soon be over. The insults of the foe are only for a moment. The Lord will soon turn their laughter into lamentation and our sighing into singing.[2]

I don't always do the right thing with my anger. But when I do allow God to fight my battles, I find evidence of His supernatural fingerprints all over the resolution of an upsetting situation—and trust me, the resolution does come. In chapter 13 I relate just such an incident. God's form of damage control is the only one I know that leaves a situation better than it was before the damage occurred. In time, if we allow God to work, relationships are restored from the ashes of the hurt. Often, when I choose to fight God's way, with love and compassion toward my enemies—instead of acting spitefully, which, admittedly, is my first impulse—I leave them with a new respect for autism-related issues. When I choose not to become aggressive and critical of them, opting instead to use gentle words of truth, my enemies often receive an awareness of the pain they've caused. They see for themselves the damage they have inflicted. This is but one of the many miraculous fingerprints of God when we pray and let Him do His work. But don't take my word for it; try it for yourself!

Here's what we know: When our children are hurt, we hurt. Cruel words crush us, but never forget that the Lord is our defender. Tell your little one that there is a God in heaven whose heart rejoices at the sound of his or her voice. Don't let the enemy fool you into thinking that God ignores the sufferings of our children. Instead, know that ours is a God of justice who will right all wrongs in His perfect timing and in His perfect way: "Do not say, I will repay evil; wait [expectantly] for the Lord, and He will rescue you" (Prov. 20:22 AMP).

Even now, when I make a mistake in life, or when I've gained a few pounds, I can hear the jeers of those neighborhood bullies yelling "Earthquake!" Yes, the scar of those hateful words has faded, yet it will forever remain. But I know that God is so much stronger than mere words. He will not ignore our pain and sorrow.

. . . .

PROMISES TO TREASURE

An end to tears

He will wipe away every tear from their eyes. Death will exist no longer; grief, crying, and pain will exist no longer, because the previous things have passed away.

—REVELATION 21:4

Comfort

Blessed and enviably happy [with a happiness produced by the experience of God's favor and especially conditioned by the revelation of His matchless grace] are those who mourn, for they shall be comforted!

—MATTHEW 5:4 (AMP)

A good outcome

That's why we can be so sure that every detail in our lives of love for God is worked into something good.

—ROMANS 8:28 (MSG)

The scale will tip in our balance

For our light and momentary troubles are achieving for us an eternal glory that far outweighs them all. So we fix our eyes not on what is seen, but on what is unseen. For what is seen is temporary, but what is unseen is eternal.

—2 CORINTHIANS 4:17–18 (NIV)

Your children are a blessing

Don't you see that children are GOD's best gift? the fruit of the womb his generous legacy? Like a warrior's fistful of arrows are the children of a vigorous youth. Oh, how blessed are you parents, with your quivers full of children! Your enemies don't stand a chance against you; you'll sweep them right off your doorstep.

—PSALM 127:3–5 (MSG)

Your Father cares for you

Aren't two sparrows sold for a penny? Yet not one of them falls to the ground without your Father's consent. But even the hairs of your head have all been counted. Don't be afraid therefore; you are worth more than many sparrows.

—MATTHEW 10:29–31

Your enemies are nothing compared to God

All who rage against you will surely be ashamed and disgraced; those who oppose you will be as nothing and perish. Though you search for your enemies, you will not find them. Those who wage war against you will be as nothing at all. For I am the LORD, your God, who takes hold of your right hand and says to you, Do not fear; I will help you.

—ISAIAH 41:11–13 (NIV)

Chapter 10

What Eye Has Not Seen nor Ear Has Heard

God's Promise of a Future

Even the most challenging and painful things that happen to us have a purpose. These children have a purpose. Without Evan, I would never have been able to see the greatness of Jenny's spirit. My daughter Jane, [as well as] Jenny, and Evan are the greatest things that ever happened to me, and learning how to love them has made me a man.

JIM CARREY

Why are there so many children who are diagnosed with an autism spectrum disorder? Whatever can God be thinking in allowing the disorder to become so prevalent? I wish I knew God's mind. But I've finally come to peace in the words of Romans 11:33: "Oh, the depth of the riches both of the wisdom and the knowledge of God! How unsearchable His judgments and untraceable His ways!" It's not for me to know the reason why so many children, including my son, live with autism.

Yet seeing the faithfulness of God in my past, I do trust Him enough to understand that—although sickness and disease were never part of His original design—He will take every sorrow life brings and turn it into something beneficial and good, something that has great worth for His children.

That's the future that God promises His children.

No one, of course, asks for pain and sorrow, and I'm no exception. Even so, every man, woman, and child will experience some level of suffering while living on this earth. This world isn't full of Andy Taylors and Barney Fifes living in Mayberry where every problem can be solved in thirty minutes. We'd like immediate answers to our predicaments, but we know that's not the reality—Mayberry is a fictional place. In real life, where pain plays out in Technicolor, every family experiences hardships that are complex and seemingly can't be fixed. If a family avoids the touch of autism, they will be grieved in other ways.

Turning from Present Pain to the Hope of Our Future

When my mother wiped away my tears after I returned home from another day of being teased at school, she'd wrap her arms around me and whisper this promise: "God has a special plan for you, Kelly." It was a simple promise, but God would not allow the hateful words of bullies to drown it out. It's a promise that stayed with me, and when life got hard I'd pull it out from the recesses of my mind and brush it off, remembering that I did, in fact, have value. I did have a God-given future. At night I'd lie in bed, the covers pulled around my head, and dream about God's mysterious plan and purpose for my life. What would it be?

It's amazing, but God's purpose for my life was planned long before I was conceived. Now that I'm grown, I see evidence of that purpose over the years of my life—my turning to God when my parents divorced, the lessons I learned from being teased, our daughter being born the perfect big sister for Alec. Yet, even now, I know I'm catching only a glimpse of the full purpose. God's purpose for me—something beneficial and good, something of great worth—is woven into a plan infinitely larger than I can see or even comprehend.

The same is true for Alec. God has a purpose for him, and this journey with autism will only strengthen it. God is faithful to do so.

Since avoiding pain entirely is impossible, take heart in knowing that we belong to One who offers to use our pain in miraculous ways for our good. God takes our sorrow and transforms it into something beautiful. When we turn from the pain and focus on God, we find strength and power to endure. But that's not all. When we've made it to the other side of a trial, we will receive the joy of knowing that we are—*thank God*—still here! We will have made it through our dark night, and we will be stronger and wiser for it.

And then something astounding will occur: our lives will emit God's radiance. Our lives will glow in confirmation—His faithfulness has now been tested and proven. We will then be filled with His light, a light that can illuminate the road of other travelers. We will have found a purpose we never knew existed—something beneficial and good, something that has great worth—and when we fulfill it, we will be rewarded with immense joy. We will find that life is an adventure, worth living.

The scars of our pain will have become our testimonies, reminding us that we have survived. Looking at them, we'll remember the strength of the One who has carried and guided us out of the valleys and up to the mountaintop. We will realize that with Christ, nothing is impossible.

> It's in Christ that we find out who we are and what we are living for. Long before we first heard of Christ and got our hopes up, he had his eye on us, had designs on us for glorious living, part of the overall purpose he is working out in everything and everyone. (Eph. 1:11–12 MSG)

Finding the Purpose in the Autism Journey

Parents, I don't believe God enjoys watching His beloved children endure the pain and sorrow of autism. I know that it grieves Him terribly, exactly like it grieves us as we watch our own children suffer. I believe that, through our experiences in parenting our children, God teaches us about some parts of His nature.

If autism is part of the equation of our lives, we have a choice to make: we can react to it in anger, bitterness, or indifference, letting it get the best of us; or we can wring the best out of it and use it. Imagine a beautiful, sun-ripened orange. Only under pressure from squeezing does it release the vitamin-rich nectar that we can drink to our health and vitality. The orange could stay on the tree and rot, never providing an ounce of benefit, or it could share its sweetness and nutrients with others. The fullness of its worth is found in giving itself to others.

It's important to understand, then, that our God is a God who wastes nothing. That's part of His mystery. He promises to turn even our deepest sorrows—even autism—to the good of our children: "We are assured and know that [God being a partner in their labor] all things work together and are [fitting into a plan] for good to and for those who love God and are called according to [His] design and purpose" (Rom. 8:28 AMP).

You've probably noticed I've been talking about this purpose in the future tense—as something yet to be fulfilled. You've probably also noticed that I've been talking about this purpose in the abstract, as something we don't yet have a clear picture of. When we're talking about the purposes of God, that's the way we have to talk. Because our purpose is ongoing, in process. You might say, "I've already found my purpose." And maybe you have. May I suggest, however, that you've found not *the* purpose, but *a* purpose, or *part* of your purpose.

The reason for our being on this earth is like a great picture puzzle, and we see that purpose only in small increments as the pieces fit together. As God places the pieces of the puzzle—our life experiences—together, a picture begins to form. Day by day, a little more of it is visible. When we look back over our years on this earth, we see that every hardship and every joy is a separate piece of the puzzle. Each experience has its own color and shape. But if we were to pick up only one piece, it would have no meaning apart from the others. As God places each piece, connecting it with the others, we see that all the pieces fit together to form one beautiful picture. As long as we are alive on this earth, however, the puzzle will never be complete because we haven't yet lived all the pieces.

Rest assured, though, that God has a plan for each and every experience in our lives whether it comes to us in joy or sorrow. The same is true in the lives of our children with autism. Have no doubt that God has a purpose for our children, one far greater than we can see right now. This purpose extends to the world around our children as they touch the lives of others. I've seen, for example, how Alec has brought out the best in me and his father, how he hones the sweetness and pa-tience of his big sister, how he nurtures generosity in his friends at school.

Is it hard for you to believe that the child you hold has a special purpose designed and crafted by Our Father long before he or she was conceived? Long before anyone spoke the word "autism" in reference to your baby, God had something special in mind for your child. Don't think for a moment that autism changes that purpose in the slightest way. *It changes nothing.* Just remember that God is able. He is able to do anything. He is able to empower our children to change the world in phenomenal ways. God is ready this very moment to take on autism, and here is the breathtaking part: His glory will shine all the more brightly through it. How? Because you know—and you will tell the news to all who ask—that you and your child could not have come so far, could not have accomplished so much, without Him.

Scripture shows us that God, in fact, chose some of the most un-likely candidates, by human standards, to be instruments for some of His most glorious acts. Let's take a look at just a few biblical heroes— God's own picks to carry out His finest work.

God's Unlikely Hero: Moses

God's people had a problem. They were in slavery to the Egyptians and were calling out for rescue. God was ready to set His people free, so He called an unlikely hero to approach the formidable Pharaoh and demand the release of the captives. God's choice for this impossible task was a runaway murderer who, interesting to note, was not gifted in speech. In fact, he stuttered. This man was Moses, who would be-come one of the greatest heroes of the Old Testament.

The Lord paid a visit to our reluctant hero in Midian to inform him that he had been handpicked to set God's people free. Moses didn't take on this task with excitement. You see, Moses had once lived in Pharaoh's palace and was well aware of the strength of his opponent. Frankly, he was intimidated and understandably so. Moses needed a lot of reassurance from God that He would go with him to complete this seemingly impossible task:

> But Moses replied to the LORD, "Please, Lord, I have never been eloquent—either in the past or recently or since You have been speaking to Your servant—because I am slow and hesitant in speech."
>
> The LORD said to him, "Who made the human mouth? Who makes him mute or deaf, seeing or blind? Is it not I, the LORD? Now go! I will help you speak and I will teach you what to say." (Exod. 4:10–12)

I overflow with gratitude when I read God's response to Moses. God was completely aware of Moses' inadequate speaking ability. After all, God had created him! Instead of allowing Moses to wallow in a puddle of self-pity, God reminded him that He was in charge, and that *no disability could keep Moses from doing God's will.*

> "I am GOD. Tell Pharaoh king of Egypt everything I say to you." And Moses answered, "Look at me. I stutter. Why would Pharaoh listen to me?" GOD told Moses, "Look at me. I'll make you as a god to Pharaoh and your brother Aaron will be your prophet. You are to speak everything I command you, and your brother Aaron will tell it to Pharaoh. Then he will release the Israelites from his land." (Exod. 6:29–7:2 MSG)

Parents, what God says here applies to autism as well. When we stop focusing on disability and focus instead on God's power, we create a place for miracles to occur. God is waiting for us to sweep away our insecurities and replace them with total reliance on Him. Sometimes it's only when we accept and acknowledge our own limitations that we learn how to be reliant on the Father. The Word of God lets us know that nothing—not even a disability—will keep our children from God's divine purpose for their lives.

God's Unlikely Hero: David

In the book of 1 Samuel, God asks His prophet Samuel to anoint a new king to replace King Saul. Saul's heart had not been fixed on the Lord, and God had someone else in mind, someone whom He would later refer to as "a man after My heart" (Acts 13:22). When God was ready to announce His choice for king, He chose an unlikely boy by the name of David. This boy would become the greatest king in the history of Israel.

God directed Samuel to seek the new king within the house of Jesse. Samuel invited Jesse to attend a sacrifice and feast. As Jesse's first son, Eliab, passed before Samuel, the prophet thought, "Surely the LORD's anointed stands here before the LORD" (1 Sam. 16:6 NIV). Samuel was making the same mistake, however, that most of us make, judging solely on the basis of outward appearance.

> But the LORD said to Samuel, "Do not consider his appearance or his height, for I have rejected him. The LORD does not look at the things man looks at. Man looks at the outward appearance, but the LORD looks at the heart." (1 Sam. 16:7 NIV)

One by one, Jesse's sons paraded before Samuel, all men of enviable strength and stature, but God did not confirm any of them to Samuel. As the prophet watched the procession, I can almost hear him thinking, *Is this the one, God? No? Surely this one, then! Huh? Not him either? Are You sure about that, God?* When seven sons had passed before Samuel, he asked Jesse, "Are these all the sons you have?" (1 Sam. 16:11 NIV).

"'There is still the youngest,' Jesse answered, 'but he is tending the sheep'" (1 Sam. 16:11 NIV). Did you catch that? Isn't it amazing that God's choice was the son whom Jesse did not even consider worthy of summoning to the feast? He wasn't even invited to the party, so to speak, but God saw a king in this young tender of sheep.

When at last David entered into Samuel's presence, God spoke up, "Rise and anoint him; he is the one" (1 Sam. 16:12 NIV).

God took that boy, overlooked by his own father, and handpicked him to rule over His people. God mowed down enemies before him, and blessed his rule. God never left David's side. At the end of his life, God told David,

> I took you from the pasture and from following the sheep, to be ruler over My people Israel. I have been with you wherever you have gone, and I have destroyed all your enemies before you. I will make a name for you like that of the greatest in the land. (1 Chron. 17:7–8)

God's promises to David were fulfilled. Now, centuries later, we still recognize the name of David—the youthful shepherd whom no one considered "king material."

Throughout Scripture, God chooses men and women whom the world has long passed by for some of His most spectacular assignments. Repeatedly, He shames the strong by empowering those whom the world deems weak and unacceptable in order to illustrate the magnitude of His glory. God's only requirement for an extraordinary kind of life is a heart, just like David's, that is fixed on Him.

Let me tell you this: God is on your side, too. When God looks at your child, a child with autism, He sees potential. God sees past any physical limitations to the inward beauty of our children. God sees their hearts, full of ability and promise. God can choose a small child to change the world. He's done it before! In using the weak, God—and only God—receives glory.

What Does This Mean for My Child?

So your child cannot speak or has limited conversation skills? You may be wondering, *How then can my child make a difference in the world?* Believe this, dear parents: your child can make a huge impact on the world.

God has a purpose for each child with autism. Society may not think that such children are up to mighty things, but God does. He will provide all they need to fulfill His unique purposes for them. God is in the business of choosing people who need His help and using them for some pretty extraordinary feats.

Remember—the visible evidence of God's power in our lives is proportional to our ability to depend on, or surrender to, Him. God empowered the apostle Paul to spread the gospel throughout the world, despite seemingly insurmountable opposition. Paul beautifully conveys the truth that God uses our weaknesses, as he tells about his own struggle with a handicap.

> Because of the extravagance of those revelations, and so I wouldn't get a big head, I was given the gift of a handicap to keep me in constant touch with my limitations. Satan's angel did his best to get me down; what he in fact did was push me to my knees. No danger then of walking around high and mighty! At first I didn't think of it as a gift, and begged God to remove it. Three times I did that, and then he told me, My grace is enough; it's all you need. My strength comes into its own in your weakness. Once I heard that, I was glad to let it happen. I quit focusing on the handicap and began appreciating the gift. It was a case of Christ's strength moving in on my weakness. (2 Cor. 12:7–9 MSG)

Has Satan been whispering into your ear that your child's purpose is lessened by autism? It's a lie! The enemy of God's people wants you to lose hope and fall into depression about your child's potential. Don't fall for it! Remember that when God has a special task to fulfill, He rarely chooses someone on the world's "Ten Most Likely to Succeed" list.

God can work through our autistic children, taking them far beyond the life we might have expected for them—and using them to change the lives of many people. Don't underestimate God's future for your child. One day, you'll find yourself recounting the story of your child's life to a new friend, amazed at how far God has taken your baby.

Empowered with the might of God, your child *can* make a difference in the lives of others. If you want proof, just look at your own life. Perhaps in loving your child you have a new ability to see the important things in life, things to which many are blind. Maybe you can see

God's divine love evident in your child's smile, something you might have missed in the wake of a "normal" life full of soccer games and sleepovers. I know that Alec has forever changed me. I'm more extroverted and assertive, more patient and compassionate, living a closer walk with God. I will never be the same, and I never want to go back to the person I was before that boy graced me with his presence.

Children with autism are like walking mirrors that reflect what truly lies in the heart of those whom they encounter. As we meet children with autism in our daily walk, our reaction to them casts back an image of our heart's condition, as if peering into a looking glass. Sometimes we don't want to see the reality of the reflection that greets us. If we ignore children with autism, walking past them as if they don't exist, or if we fail to respond to their cries, then we won't like what we see in that mirror. If we extend a hand to help, or offer a shoulder to carry their burdens, or wipe away their tears, we will see another image in the looking glass. When we react to them in love, we look into their mirror and see the image of Christ.

I know that Alec is going to cause people to face several truths about life that they might not want to face. Maybe some of those people will, having known my son, choose to love rather than hate, to help rather than hurt, to lift up rather than pull down. I know our children are going to do far more than we can dream. They will see miraculous, wonderful, God-given victories that will have glorious significance in heaven, if not on earth.

I think our children are going to change the world! Our children, God's unlikely heroes, will alter it for the better. I hope and pray that I will be here to see it.

Promises to Treasure

Weakness can be strength
But God chose the foolish things of the world to shame the wise;
God chose the weak things of the world to shame the strong.
—1 Corinthians 1:27 (NIV)

God has always known us

Your eyes saw me when I was formless; all [my] days were written in Your book and planned before a single one of them began.

—Psalm 139:16

God has a plan for us

"For I know the plans I have for you"—[this is] the LORD's declaration—"plans for [your] welfare, not for disaster, to give you a future and a hope."

—Jeremiah 29:11

The Spirit will show you God's will

Do not conform any longer to the pattern of this world, but be transformed by the renewing of your mind. Then you will be able to test and approve what God's will is—his good, pleasing and perfect will.

—Romans 12:2 (niv)

Chapter 11

Strength for the Weary Heart

God's Promise of Sufficiency

We are pressured in every way but not crushed; we are perplexed but not in despair; we are persecuted but not abandoned; we are struck down but not destroyed.

2 Corinthians 4:8–9

The year is 2004, not long before Alec was diagnosed with autism. I'm sitting on the curb next to our Big Green Van, in the parking lot behind Alec's preschool. I'm holding a pizza in one hand and plates, napkins, drinks, and an overloaded diaper bag in the other. It's a beautiful spring day. "A fine day," as we Southerners say, "for a picnic." The birds are singing, the sun is warm, and the air is fragrant with the scent of the freshly mowed lawn. Muffled laughter floats to my ears as children romp in the inflated Moon Bounce on the front lawn of the preschool.

Here I sit, pleading once again with Alec to get out of the van. Alec, however, is in rare form today, repeatedly refusing to leave his protected, quiet space. Each time I try to coax him out, he kicks me—and hard. My pint-sized Tasmanian Devil is clinging to his car seat as if his life depended on it. In case you've never tried to wrestle an angry Tasmanian Devil out of a van while holding on to a hot pizza, drinks, plates, napkins, cups, and a diaper bag, I don't recommend it.

This is the way Alec is ending his first year at his church preschool— and what a fitting end to an exasperating year. I'm annoyed with Matt, who was supposed to meet us in the parking lot fifteen minutes ago. That anger acts as a buffer to my real pain: the growing awareness that I can't control my own toddler, and the shame that I am a mother who can't manage to get her son out of a van without assistance. I look around for help, but everyone is already seated on blankets in the distance, too far away to notice my distress.

I quit! A thought directed at God. *I can't do this anymore!*

I'd spent one too many embarrassing days carrying my angry boy over my shoulder, his little fists pounding my back as we maneuvered our way out of the preschool. Alec's constant tantrums had worn me down. There was nothing left in my reserves, no fuel to keep me going. Nothing, so far, was working, and no one was able to handle my son. Not his teachers. Not my husband. Not even me.

God, this is too hard! I can't do this! I drop the diaper bag, the plates, the cups, and the drinks and lay the pizza box on the curb. Then I rest my face in my hands and cry. We're a sight, Alec and me, stranded in the preschool parking lot, both an emotional mess.

Suddenly, there's a tap on my shoulder. I turn and see Matt, who in one motion sweeps me to my feet; takes the pizza, the drinks, and the diaper bag with one arm; in a second swoop, he hoists my son from the van.

"Where have you been?" I snap, choosing to attack the man who's just saved my day, rather than kiss his sweet hand (which would have been a much better choice).

"I've been here, Kelly," Matt calmly responds to my hysteria. "I was parked in the front lot looking for you for the past twenty-five minutes. I finally drove around to the back parking lot to see if you were here."

For the next several minutes I take my frustrations out on my precious husband, who's done nothing wrong. Matt, though, has a special ability to sense when I'm standing on an emotional cliff and is careful not to give me a reason to jump. He takes my berating in silence, uttering an occasional "I know." He gently deposits Alec on the blanket and walks over to greet the teachers.

Days later when the emotional wounds of the picnic disaster began to fade, I realized that God had sent me a hero that day—a hero I acrimoniously attacked. God had worked through Matt to rescue me from the curb and carry me through that day's trial.

Broken Marriages and Autism

During the frenzied search for information about autism in the months following Alec's diagnosis, I discovered a community of parents willing to share nuggets of wisdom with me. To this day, I'm thankful for these dedicated parents who took time out of their busy days to speak with me. You can find parents such as these serving on autism boards or supporting each other in autism discussion groups throughout the community and even online (see appendix A). I have no idea how they do it, given the substantial responsibilities they carry at home, but they do, and I'm grateful for them.

In those early weeks I made contact with another mother in North Carolina, who was willing to share her knowledge of autism with me. I had many concerns and questions for her about therapies, education requirements, and funding. She provided the names of places to go for help, and she gave information to me that got me started in biomedical therapies for Alec. I remember feeling a sense of relief as I spoke with this woman, that is, until she gave me an ominous word of warning that I remember to this day.

Almost as an afterthought, she said, "Prepare for your marriage to fall apart."

A shudder went through me as I considered her alarming words. *How could she say such a terrible thing to me? Certainly she is overreacting!*

But there's an unfortunate truth in her warning. Many autistic organizations do estimate a higher than average divorce rate among couples caring for an autistic child. The rate of marriage failure in families caring for a child with special needs, although varied according to the source, can be as high as 80 percent.[1]

My new friend's warning scared me. I thought about my day at the preschool picnic when I directed my frustrations at Matt, even after he rescued me from the situation. Was our marriage in danger of becoming a statistic now that we had a child with a special need?

The truth was, I *had* been picking fights with Matt. All too often I chose to complain, focus on negative issues, and whine. *I'm doing so much more for Alec than Matt is! Why isn't Matt carrying more of the burden?*

Then I realized I was guilty of something that could cost me my marriage: I was relying on Matt, rather than God, to be my primary source of strength. God says in His Word, "Do not fear, for I am with you; do not be afraid, for I am your God. I will strengthen you; I will help you; I will hold on to you with My righteous right hand" (Isa. 41:10).

Matt hadn't issued a single complaint, but I knew I needed to make a change and unload my spiritual burdens to God instead of over-burdening my husband. I can't expect Matt to replenish me when my fuel gauge is on empty. I can't expect Matt to be a constant source of happiness, because he gets tired, too. He's carrying the weight of paying for Alec's care along with meeting the spiritual and emotional needs of our family. In all honesty, it's often Matt, the father and head of our family, whose needs are overlooked. I am so blessed to have him in this battle with me.

My new friend correctly warned me that marriages with heavy fam-ily responsibilities are burdened. She was incorrect, though, in saying that my marriage was doomed . . . at least that's what is sounded like to me. I am certain of one thing: providing for a child with autism certainly tests a marriage, but God can help keep it intact. When both partners hold fast to each other with one hand and to God with the other, hardships such as ours, instead of disassembling a family, can serve as a glue that binds a couple closer. Marriages work best when they are a union of three: "If someone overpowers one person, two can resist him. A cord of three strands is not easily broken" (Eccl. 4:12).

When life drains you, remember that only God provides true re-freshment, the living water, needed to survive a battle with autism. Go to Him first, uniting with your spouse in prayer for your child and ask-ing God to bind your marriage in compassionate, forgiving love.

So many wedding ceremonies include the text from 1 Corinthians 13, often referred to as the "Love" chapter. Paul's words have become so familiar to most of us that we no longer actually hear them, failing to be challenged by the words describing the essence of true love. When spouses choose—and it is a choice—to love each other as described in 1 Corinthians 13, the marriage will succeed. I'm thankful that God gently reminds me when I have failed to love Matt with the kind of love found in Paul's words, and enables me to make a change. We have no power over our spouses, but we can personally choose to love them in the manner expressed in the "Love" chapter:

> Love never gives up. Love cares more for others than for self. Love doesn't want what it doesn't have. Love doesn't strut, doesn't have a swelled head, doesn't force itself on others, isn't always "me first," doesn't fly off the handle, doesn't keep score of the sins of others, doesn't revel when others grovel, takes pleasure in the flowering of truth, puts up with anything, trusts God always, always looks for the best, never looks back, but keeps going to the end. (1 Cor. 13:4–7 MSG)

This kind of love is our best chance at beating the odds of divorce and having a marriage that is actually strengthened—instead of destroyed—by autism.

"What If . . . ?": When Panic Sets In

What if your marriage is in danger of failure, sinking under the weight of bitterness, blame, and weariness? Or what if you're a single parent? What if you're fighting the battle of autism on your own? What if you've run out of money to help your child, gasping for air in a tide of rising debt? What if you don't know what to do next and want to give up at this very moment? What if you feel the walls closing in on you, pressing with responsibilities far too great, and you feel the air being squeezed out of your lungs?

Lift up your head, dear friend, and let me tell you a story.

A few years ago, my husband had a conference in Boston and I decided to travel with him. Both lovers of history, we were excited to walk Boston's Freedom Trail on one of Matt's free days. After walking along the gorgeous harbor, we came to the Bunker Hill Monument, a granite obelisk standing 221 feet high on the site of the first major battle of the American Revolution. Matt grabbed my hand and walked up the hill to the monument entrance, eager to climb the interior steps to see the grand view from the top.

Oh, how I wanted to soak in the view of the harbor from the lookout of that monument! I wanted to go inside and march up the stairway to touch the sky, just like Matt wanted, but I had a problem: I'm claustrophobic. I stood at the entrance and slowly tilted my head back to see the peak of the monument. The walls of the monument tapered as they rose toward the sky and the few windows provided only dim light for the ascent.

At this point, I had a choice to make: stay on the ground and only dream of the view, or say a prayer and place my foot on the first step. Gripping Matt's hand like a vice, I took a deep breath and with a silent prayer headed up the stairway.

Matt and I began to climb the spiraling stairs; with each step the walls grew closer and closer. Tourists passed by us as they made their descent, oblivious to my fear. My chest tightened with each step, and I felt the beginnings of a panic attack. *What was I thinking? What view is worth this fear?*

My mind raced. *What if I lose it in this monument? What if they have to carry me back down, a crazy, hyperventilating woman?*

I turned to make a bolt back down the stairs, but a crowd of tourists blocked the way down. I reached out and touched the walls, which were closing in on me. The air was heavy and still. What could I do?

Pray! Oh, yes, I will pray my way to the top of this monument! Focusing on one step at a time, keeping my thoughts on God's ability to get me there, I tried to ignore the walls closing in. My internal monologue went something like this: *Step, step, focus on God! Step, step, the walls! I need air! I can't do this! No! Focus on God, focus on God! Step, step, focus!*

At last I placed my foot on the top step—and do you know what? Sunlight flooded around me. An exhilarating view of Boston Harbor stretched out before me. My every sense—sight, smell, even my breath flowing through my lungs and the beating of my heart—drank it all in, and all of it thrilled me! It was worth the fear, worth the effort to be strengthened in the knowledge of what I could achieve when I focused only on my sufficiently able God, the great I AM.

I've tucked this moment of victory into my heart, and whenever I'm overwhelmed by the responsibilities of autism, I find strength in doing what I did in Boston: taking each step individually and focusing not on my situation but on God's strength and power.

We parents are called to lead our autistic children up into the sunshine. As you climb, remember that God is always there with you, empowering you to do the work He has called you to do. If you keep your hand firmly in His, if you keep climbing, taking one step at a time, when you get to the top you'll find that God has something very special for you—the life that He intended for your child. Paul writes,

> For our light, momentary affliction (this slight distress of the passing hour) is ever more and more abundantly preparing and producing and achieving for us an everlasting weight of glory [beyond all measure, excessively surpassing all comparisons and all calculations, a vast and transcendent glory and blessedness never to cease!], since we consider and look not to the things that are seen but to the things that are unseen; for the things that are visible are temporal (brief and fleeting), but the things that are invisible are deathless and everlasting. (2 Cor. 4:17–18 AMP)

Laying Every Burden Down

Parents, make no mistake—in this war against autism we are in the fight of our lives, and victory isn't going to be easy. But the reward is your child living the best life he or she can possibly have. Never give up. Keep going, keep reaching, keep walking, and keep praying.

There are times when the battle gets ugly: off days, bullies, insensitive adults, immovable bureaucracies, overdrawn bank accounts. We want to raise the white flag and surrender. Our foe, autism, threatens to rob us of the blessings that God intends for our families—blessings like peace of mind, a restful home, and time to treasure the simple things of life, enjoying our children who, Scripture tells us, are "a heritage from the LORD" and a "reward" (Ps. 127:3).

It's a daily struggle to keep up with the therapies and the finances, your child's brain chemistry and special diets. Each day we need to ask for help—help from individuals, from organizations, and especially from God. It takes great humility to ask for help when we'd prefer to handle everything ourselves. Asking for help is hard, but dealing with autism in your own strength is harder.

When you're ready to throw in the towel, remember the words of Jesus: "Come to Me, all of you who are weary and burdened, and I will give you rest. All of you, take up My yoke and learn from Me, because I am gentle and humble in heart, and you will find rest for yourselves" (Matt. 11:28–29).

What does it mean to come to Jesus with our burdens and weariness? For me, it means getting up early and asking God to direct my day, asking Him to remove all obstacles—external and internal—that will keep me from His will for me. It's asking Him to show me what is really important, to shut my mind to fear and worries—about money or my child's future—fears that keep me focused on autism instead of Him. It's asking for forgiveness for the wrongs committed yesterday, and truly accepting His renewed mercies for the day ahead. It's forgiving myself, too, knowing that I've been forgiven by God.

I ask God for wisdom as I seek to understand my son, and to find the best doctors, therapies, and educators for my son's specific needs. I ask God for friends for Alec who will encircle him, for understanding adults to guide him, and I ask for the physical energy to be the mother he needs. I pray that God protects and seals my marriage, asking for God to help me love Matt the way God loves me.

I thank God, too, for the progress Alec has made. I thank Him for the hugs, the love, the smiles, and the laughter he gives. I thank Him for a warm bed to lay Alec down in at night. I thank Him for my family. I thank Him for the air I breathe. I thank Him for all that this journey is teaching me.

When do we need to lay our burdens at Jesus' feet? Every day! Only then can we experience life abundantly, the life of freedom that Jesus offers us. When we do, God replaces our anxieties with a supernatural peace and supplies everything we need for the day at hand. Scripture says,

> Don't worry about anything, but in everything, through prayer and petition with thanksgiving, let your requests be

made known to God. And the peace of God, which surpasses every thought, will guard your hearts and your minds in Christ Jesus. (Phil. 4:6–7)

I have to be honest with you; the hardest part for me is walking away from my burdens after I've placed them at the cross. How often I want to hang on to my burdens, wrestling one from God's hand so I can stew over it, as though worry could solve a single one of my problems. I offer God suggestions of my own, as if I possess more wisdom than He. I stoop down to retrieve a concern or two, feeling lost without its familiar weight around my shoulders, and before I know it, I'm bent over, stressed out, and irritable. So back to the cross I go! I let the tears fall for a moment and release my cares again, saying, "Here they are, God, all of my needs, hopes, and desires. I've made a mess of them. But they're Yours now."

When I finally walk away, He whispers to me, "I've got them. All of them. Just watch Me work . . ."

Autism Is No Match for the Power of Jesus' Love

Raising a child with autism is one of the great storms of life. God never promised that our lives would be without storms. What He has promised is that He will be sufficient in the storms. They will not consume us: "I have told you these things, so that in me you may have peace. In this world you will have trouble. But take heart! I have overcome the world" (John 16:33 NIV).

Read that precious promise again. If you have a child with autism, certainly you and your child will have your share of trouble in life. There will be bills to pay, educational challenges, difficult social situations. But whatever the trouble, whatever the storm, Jesus tells us to be encouraged, because He has *already* overcome the world—including autism.

Take heart that you and your child rest in the arms of Someone who knows everything about each of you. He knows your fears, your needs, your inabilities, your wants and desires, your lonely times, your frustrations, every tear you've cried and every rock on your path. He knows everything about the mysteries of autism itself!

Here's the promise to you: nothing—no situation, disability, or need—no, *nothing at all* is too big to stand against Jesus!

Promises to Treasure

Rest

Come to Me, all you who labor and are heavy-laden and over-burdened, and I will cause you to rest. [I will ease and relieve and refresh your souls.] Take My yoke upon you and learn of Me, for I am gentle (meek) and humble (lowly) in heart, and you will find rest (relief and ease and refreshment and recreation and blessed quiet) for your souls.

—Matthew 11:28–29 (amp)

Joy

Now if we are children, then we are heirs—heirs of God and co-heirs with Christ, if indeed we share in his sufferings in order that we may also share in his glory. I consider that our present sufferings are not worth comparing with the glory that will be revealed in us.

—Romans 8:17–18 (niv)

Provision

But seek first the kingdom of God and His righteousness, and all these things will be provided for you. Therefore don't worry about tomorrow, because tomorrow will worry about itself. Each day has enough trouble of its own.

—Matthew 6:33–34

Competence

Not that we are competent in ourselves to claim anything for ourselves, but our competence comes from God. He has made us competent as ministers of a new covenant—not of the letter but of the Spirit; for the letter kills, but the Spirit gives life.

—2 Corinthians 3:5–6 (NIV)

Grace

And God is able to make every grace overflow to you, so that in every way, always having everything you need, you may excel in every good work. As it is written: He has scattered; He has given to the poor; His righteousness endures forever.

—2 Corinthians 9:8–9

Help from the Lord

Wait and hope for and expect the Lord; be brave and of good courage and let your heart be stout and enduring. Yes, wait for and hope for and expect the Lord.

—Psalm 27:14 (AMP)

Strength

He gives strength to the weary and strengthens the powerless. Youths may faint and grow weary, and young men stumble and fall, but those who trust in the LORD will renew their strength; they will soar on wings like eagles; they will run and not grow weary; they will walk and not faint.

—Isaiah 40:29–31

An oasis in the desert

The poor and the needy seek water, but there is none; their tongues are parched with thirst. I, the LORD, will answer them; I, the God of Israel, do not forsake them. I will open rivers on the barren heights, and springs in the middle of the plains. I will turn the desert into a pool of water and dry land into springs of water. I will plant cedars in the desert, acacias, myrtles, and olive trees. I will put cypress trees in the desert, elms and box trees together, so that all may see and know, consider and understand, that the hand of the LORD has done this, the Holy One of Israel has created it.

—Isaiah 41:17–20

Chapter 12

From Speechless to Unspeakable Joy

God's Promise of Joy

Rejoice in the Lord always. I will say it again: Rejoice!
PHILIPPIANS 4:4 (NIV)

Those who sow in tears will reap with shouts of joy.
PSALM 126:5

"Isn't it remarkable that a four-year-old can swim so well?"

These were the words of a mother sitting next to me at our neighborhood pool. She was watching her son, only a few months older than Alec, in the midst of a swimming lesson in three-foot deep water. I shot a quick glance behind me to the kiddy pool and located Alec. He was studying a bug floating in the foot-deep water.

"Yes, it is." I nodded, with a big fake smile. "Remarkable."

Being around other neurotypical kids is sometimes hard, isn't it? It takes effort not to compare the milestones of that child to your child's developmental delays. I've found tremendous joy in seeing Alec improve over the years, and I'm thrilled by his remarkable progress . . . that is until I see another child of his age doing something that my son can't begin to master, and I'm reminded of the long road ahead.

I spent many afternoons that year watching other four-year-olds learn to swim. They splashed around the pool to the "ooh's" and "aah's" of their mothers with each new skill. In the beginners' class they blew bubbles as instructed and kicked their legs behind them. In a few weeks, they were swimming.

And I was envious.

At four, Alec was one of the oldest kids in the kiddy pool. I would have loved to enroll him in a beginners' swimming class, but he couldn't respond to the spoken instructions. Not only that, but Alec was extremely timid in deeper water. My boy loved to sit in the baby pool, but he clamped on to my shoulders with the strength of Samson whenever I managed to float him out to the big pool.

My daughter, Elise, has an extraordinary relationship with her little brother, which is one of the greatest blessings God has given to us. I don't know where I'd be without her ability to talk with Alec, to calm him down, and to teach him how to be a kid. Long after she outgrew her arm "floaties," as we called them, she convinced Alec to roll them up his arms. He was so proud to wear his bright orange hand-me-downs from his wise and wonderful big sister.

One day not long after that Alec took my hand and walked me to the big pool. This meant one of two things: he wanted to sit on the steps and splash or he wanted me to walk him around in the water with his arms wrapped in a stranglehold around my neck.

That day a zillion kids were laughing and splashing around the shallow end. The noise would terrorize any kid with a sensory integration disorder, and it even made me cringe a few times, but we stepped into the water anyway.

Alec held on tightly as we entered the water. "Give me a hug!" he said, using one of his favorite scripted phases in a semiappropriate way. (Translation: "Let me hold on to your neck so I'll feel safe!") From time to time, I balanced him on my knee, pulling his arms away from my neck so I could take in a breath of air. Once, after he got comfortable with the bouncing, I floated him away from me holding only his hands. Immediately, a look of sheer terror crossed his face, but soon a flash of timid joy replaced it. A few minutes passed and then I wrenched one of my hands out of his viselike grasp. Another look of terror was soon replaced by a smile. I heaped mounds of praise on my son, encouraging him to say, "Look at me! I can do it!"

Finally, I pulled my other hand away, leaving Alec supported only by the arm floaties.

He gasped in fright, and, seeing his fear, I had an immediate urge to take him back into my arms. Something made me hesitate, though, and as I did, his face changed, his fear replaced by an expression of pure joy. He was doing it! He was on his own, floating on the water, eyes bright with a new confidence. Alec was "swimming" in the big pool with all of the big kids, doing what they do. In that moment, my boy was flying solo.

I can't tell you what I felt at that moment, seeing my son understand his own ability and no longer afraid. Within minutes he was moving around the pool in his floaties, going to the steps to jump in again and again, lost in the euphoria of a child experiencing something in life for the very first time.

The other moms at the pool must have thought I was insane—given the amount of praise I lavished on my son as he splashed into the water sporting his bright orange floaties. But how could I not?

I thought, *I am so like Alec. If I would only let go, what could I achieve? Could I push past my fears and discover joy that I have never known? Could I achieve more than I think I can?* Alec floated on the water, a huge smile shining on his wet cheeks. I couldn't help but share his joy.

God wants so much more for us, and more for our children. But we hold on tightly to our fears, fears that keep us from doing the incredible. It's important to note that Alec was never in danger, because I was with him, even as God is with us so we have nothing to fear. When we abide in His presence, we receive joy. Sometimes He pushes us off into unknown territory to take us to a better place, a promised land. When we let go of our fears, choosing to trust Him fully, we swim the deeper waters to the kind of life that Jesus wants us to have: "I have come that they may have life, and have it to the full" (John 10:10 NIV).

Joy: Fact or Fallacy?

Parents, joy and happiness are not one and the same. Happiness is a feeling entirely dependent on one's situation in life. It's fleeting and subject to the world around us. Autism can crush the feeling of happiness.

Joy, however, is something entirely different. The *Holman Illustrated Bible Dictionary* defines joy as a "state of delight and well being that results from knowing and serving God."[1] Think about that. Joy is not simply pasting on a smile, but rather a state of being, that is the fruit of knowing and serving God. And it fills us to the brim with content-ment and delight. Joy enables us to soar above autism and live the life God intended for us. Doing so may seem like an impossible dream, but I promise you, it is not.

You and your child can live lives of joy—even in the midst of autism—and in fact, this is exactly what Jesus wants for you. In John 10:10, Jesus tells us that He left the heavens so that we can have a joyful and abun-dant life no matter our current circumstances.

This state of joy is not a fallacy or some pie-in-the-sky ideal; it is a reality, exemplified in the life of Paul. After he was illegally arrested, then beaten, publicly humiliated, and imprisoned, he wrote these words: "I know both how to have a little, and I know how to have a lot. In any and all circumstances I have learned the secret [of being con-tent]—whether well-fed or hungry, whether in abundance or in need. I am able to do all things through Him who strengthens me" (Phil. 4:12–13).

Yes, Paul had the secret, all right! Paul's hardships were never able to steal his joy, nor, for that matter, the song from his lips. His "secret" enabled him to sing while sitting in the dark stench of a Roman prison (see Acts 16:25).

Abiding in Christ: The Secret to Joy

But wait! I sense some scoffing out there! *No way*, you might be thinking. *How is this possible when autism has robbed my child of so much? How can I have joy with such a loss?*

You need to know that we can't manufacture joy ourselves. Joy, Scripture says, is a gift, a supernatural blessing from God, referred to as a "fruit of the Spirit":

> But the fruit of the [Holy] Spirit [the work which His presence within accomplishes] is love, joy (gladness), peace, patience (an even temper, forbearance), kindness, goodness (benevolence), faithfulness, gentleness (meekness, humility), self-control (self-restraint, continence). Against such things there is no law [that can bring a charge]. (Gal. 5:22–23 AMP)

Joy is promised to us when we live our lives—or abide—within the love of Christ.

Remember the "Living Water" we talked about in chapter 4? The Living Water is the promised Helper, the Holy Spirit, our great Advocate and Comforter. When we surrender to the Spirit's guidance on a daily basis—in other words, when we live by the Spirit and do not hinder His work in our lives—then we receive the fruits of the Spirit.

Joy, dear parents, is a fruit of the Spirit. It's a gift that comes as we walk with Christ. As Warren Wiersbe writes,

> The secret of Christian joy is to believe what God says in His Word and act upon it. Faith that isn't based on the Word is not faith at all; it is presumption or superstition. Joy that isn't the result of faith is not joy at all; it is only a "good feeling" that will soon disappear. Faith based on the Word will produce joy that will weather the storms of life.[2]

Jesus wants us to have lives of joy. In a straightforward way, without symbolic terms or complex spiritual themes, He explains how to have joy in our lives right now:

> As the Father has loved me, so have I loved you. Now remain in my love. If you obey my commands, you will remain in my love, just as I have obeyed my Father's commands and remain in his love. I have told you this so that my joy may be in you and that your joy may be complete. My command is this: Love each other as I have loved you. Greater love has no one than this, that he lay down his life for his friends. (John 15:9–13 NIV)

When I read His words, something wonderful grabs me: parents of exceptional children have the opportunity of knowing the "greater love" that exists. We'd give anything to see our children restored. As Christ laid down His life for sinners, so we lay down our lives for our children—in tears, prayers, finances, even our entire being. In doing so, we receive the priceless blessing of knowing the greatest love there is. Wrap your mind around what that means! The world searches for love and significance. Our lives, as parents of children with autism, *are* significant. We can understand the heart of Christ for His people because it's the same love that exists within us as we hold our child with autism. What a blessing to experience that kind of love!

Beware the Enemies of Joy!

True spiritual joy, then, is a gift, a fruit (or result of) living within the love of Christ. This supernatural joy is actually a strength (Neh. 8:10). It gives us spiritual power to overcome anything life throws at us, including autism. We also now know that we must abide in Christ's love to hold on to that joy.

But look out! Satan, the enemy of God, has prepared a lineup of temptations with the sole purpose of trying to rob us of the spiritual joy that Jesus gives. God's Word warns us about this: "Be sober! Be on the alert! Your adversary the Devil is prowling around like a roaring lion, looking for anyone he can devour. Resist him, firm in the faith, knowing that the same sufferings are being experienced by your brothers in the world" (1 Peter 5:8–9).

Allow me to present three enemies of joy, disguised as temptations that parents must face on a daily basis. If we learn to recognize them as enemies, we'll be able quickly to put a stop to their antics before our gift of joy is stolen away.

Enemy of Joy #1: The Coveter

Why do you think God placed the sin of coveting, or desiring what someone else has, on his Big Ten list of commandments (Exod. 20:17)? I can give you two reasons: (1) we are created for God and only God; (2) for our protection. It's there to help us hold on to joy.

Moms and dads of ASD children are especially vulnerable to the attack of this enemy. Each day, we're surrounded by healthy, happy children. We listen in silence as other parents share tales of track meets, softball scores, dance recitals, trophies, ribbons, and honor rolls. Americans, especially, take a great interest in the achievements of their children and love to share them with other parents.

But *we* have stories of successes, too! We're thrilled when our child verbalizes a complex sentence, or when we say goodbye to diapers at long last! I, for one, would do a back handspring if my son would put one, just one, vegetable into his mouth! We can—and should—experience joy in these victories each day, but so often we compare them with the accolades given to our neighbor's child.

Who decides whether one success is greater than another? Did your child work hard to learn to write his name, or complete a school report? You bet she did! How long did it take for your child to ride a bike? Years? These are monumental victories, but the enemy tells us they're insignificant. This is a lie. Don't believe it! Refuse to compare the unique gifts God gives to you and your child with those He gives to another child. It's a trap that leads to bitterness.

Enemy of Joy #2: The Grump

In the morning before my feet hit the ground, I hear two voices in my head. The first one I will call "The Grump." The Grump has nothing good to say. The Grump loves to remind me of the reasons I should pull the covers over my head and stay in bed.

You have an IEP meeting at school today, remember? I don't think you've prepared enough![3] Strangely, The Grump's voice sounds just like mine! *They're going to walk all over you, you know.* The Grump wants me to dwell on things I'd rather forget. *I see that little Billy Anderson is having his birthday party today. Hmm. He must be the same age as Alec. All of the other kids on the street will be going, no doubt. How rude to leave out your son.* I'm thinking Alec will be hurt, but it really feels more like I'm the one who's hurt.

I hate The Grump. But I love the other voice. I'll call this one "The Blessed." The words of The Blessed flow something like this: *Wow, another day! God, I wonder where You are going to show up today. You know that IEP meeting we have? Well, I know that You're going with me, even before me, right into that meeting to prepare the way for Alec to receive the services he needs. God, You promise in Scripture that You will provide for Alec. Thank You, Father! So I'm walking into that meeting as a child of God, okay? Let's go!*

The Blessed sees the good in people around me: *It was really sweet of the neighbor boy to shoot some hoops with Alec yesterday. I'll be sure to mention it to him next time I see him. I'm thankful Lord, that it made Alec feel so great, so included.* The Blessed finds the good that God brings and remembers to thank Him for His goodness and provision. This is praise.

Let's face it: it's easier to listen to The Grump instead of The Blessed. But don't! Doing so robs us of our daily joy. The Grump wants to feed on your soul, sucking up your hope that your family will rise above autism. The Blessed knows that God is more powerful than autism, and urges you to praise God right now, expecting great things for your child.

Praise is one of the most powerful weapons that God gives to us. Scripture tells us that praise has the power to relieve a heavy spirit (Isa. 61:3 AMP). In my own life, I believe that surrounding myself in praise to God is the one reason I haven't fallen into depression. When I'm at the end of my rope, I put on a praise and worship CD and meditate on the words. I don't wait to feel the emotion of gratitude. I make a choice to be grateful.

In the book of Philippians, Paul, writing from prison, shares another secret to joy: "Finally brothers, whatever is true, whatever is honorable, whatever is just, whatever is pure, whatever is lovely, whatever is commendable—if there is any moral excellence and if there is any praise—dwell on these things" (Phil. 4:8).

Praise is a vitally important element in knowing and serving God and in helping parents to maintain joy in the face of autism. It provides the lift, the air, to allow us to fly above autism's attempt to pull us down.

Enemy of Joy #3: The Time Traveler

Alec and Elise call me upstairs to share the latest *Captain Underpants* adventure book with them. Although I admit to an enjoyment of infantile humor, I can't take the time to stop my writing just now. There's a work deadline tomorrow, the laundry needs to be moved to the dryer, my in-laws are coming over for dinner and I don't know what to fix . . . yada, yada, yada. My children, however, are relentless, so I go. But I make sure that, even though I don't say a word, each footfall on the stairs registers enough vibration to show my irritation.

Once upstairs, Alec sits down with the book and begins to read. I can hear that his reading has really improved. *Wow, he's doing great,* I think as I listen to my boy perfectly sound out the word "toilet." *I can't believe how much he's learned this year and . . . wait, did I remember to send in that insurance form yesterday? No, I didn't, and I'll bet I need to run to the post office to get some more stamps before I can. Maybe I'll go tomorrow after I finish the laundry and finish that project for my client, and . . .*

Suddenly, Alec is done and the moment is gone forever. It was a perfect opportunity for joy, but I chose to ponder tomorrow's trip to the post office instead.

Right now, God is serving up a plateful of joy for you, an opportunity to know Him and serve Him by showing love to others. But you have to stop and take it. Focus on the moment that God gives to you, and don't spend your days dreaming of the past or worrying about the future. This is the only today you'll ever have. "Give your entire attention to what God is doing right now, and don't get worked up about what may or may not happen tomorrow. God will help you deal with whatever hard things come up when the time comes" (Matt. 6:34 MSG).

Ain't No Joy Like the Joy of Being Redeemed

I'd be negligent if I failed to include the ultimate joy—that of knowing we have been redeemed and rescued by Jesus. Out of all the joys, there is none like the joy that comes from redemption. Think of it: a lost person found. A ransom paid and a captive set free. A sinner's sins not only forgiven, but forgotten. The sick healed. The child lost to a world of autism, rescued.

No words can ever adequately express the magnitude and level of that joy. When it is realized—the captive free, the kidnapped child of God ransomed—the soul finally, perhaps after years of doubt, realizes its own value and worth in being ransomed for so great a price. Consider this: even the heavenly angels do not experience redemption. I imagine them regarding us with a childlike awe, wondering how it must feel to comprehend that there is a God who loves us so much!

Yes, that is joy, and it's ours to own . . . forever.

Advice from the Apostle Paul

As we've already seen, the apostle Paul provides an amazing example of a life overflowing in holy joy, a joy proven in the face of such adversities as loneliness, calamity, imprisonment, pain, and disability, to name only a few. The following is a sampling of his advice to us about how to have joy from knowing and serving God:

+ Be like-minded with Christ (Phil. 2:2)
+ Obey God's Word (Phil. 2:12)
+ Resist complaining (Phil. 2:14)
+ Watch out for those who would steal your joy (Phil. 3:2)
+ Keep walking with God, pressing on to take hold of His promises for you (Phil. 3:12)
+ Rejoice! (Phil. 4:4–7)
+ Meditate on the good around you (Phil. 4:8)
+ Remember that you can do all things through Christ (Phil. 4:13)

Clearly, Paul was a man who knew how to be content. We can be thankful that he wasn't satisfied merely to live an exceptional life on his own. Instead, he lived to share what he had learned with us. His written letters in the New Testament provide a priceless blueprint that teaches us how to build this exceptional kind of life for ourselves.

Promises to Treasure

Truth

I have no greater joy than this: to hear that my children are walking in the truth.

—3 John 1:4

Joy

And the ransomed of the Lord shall return and come to Zion with singing, and everlasting joy shall be upon their heads; they shall obtain joy and gladness, and sorrow and sighing shall flee away.

—Isaiah 35:10 (amp)

Peace

Rejoice in the Lord always. I will say it again: Rejoice! Let your gentleness be evident to all. The Lord is near. Do not be anxious about anything, but in everything, by prayer and petition, with thanksgiving, present your requests to God. And the peace of God, which transcends all understanding, will guard your hearts and your minds in Christ Jesus.

—Philippians 4:4–7 (niv)

Delight

The LORD your God is among you, a warrior who saves. He will rejoice over you with gladness. He will bring [you] quietness with His love. He will delight in you with shouts of joy.

—Zephaniah 3:17

Gladness

But let all who take refuge in you be glad; let them ever sing for joy. Spread your protection over them, that those who love your name may rejoice in you.

—Psalm 5:11 (niv)

Contentment

Your life should be free from the love of money. Be satisfied with what you have, for He Himself has said, I will never leave you or forsake you.

—HEBREWS 13:5

Chapter 13

Speaking Out for the Speechless
Offering God's Promises to Others

Then He took a child, had him stand among them, and taking him in His arms, He said to them, "Whoever welcomes one little child such as this in My name welcomes Me. And whoever welcomes Me does not welcome Me, but Him who sent Me."
MARK 9:36–37

"That kid is *so* disruptive! I will *not* have him in our classroom!"

I'd just met "Sharon" at a gathering of mothers to work on our scrapbooks. Our host, "Gail," a friend of mine, was scarlet-cheeked as she realized that her friend Sharon was about to launch a new—and uncomfortable—topic of conversation. Gail had started a part-time business as a scrapbooking consultant. I'd offered to her the Langston family mountain house to take a group of her clients and spend a relaxing weekend archiving memories.

We'd gathered around a long table, chatting it up as we sorted our photographs—children in football uniforms, at swim meets, and at Walt Disney World. The light conversation centered on children and family as usual.

When the topic of discussion turned toward schooling, Sharon suddenly began to vent about a certain child who was creating a stir in her son's classroom. My heart jumped and I slumped down in my chair, expecting more to come. And, of course, you know that it did.

Sharon detailed her recent conversations with her son's teacher about a particular child in the classroom. The level of displeasure in her tone sent a chill up my spine.

"I told her, '*That kid* is so disruptive! I will not have *him* in my son's classroom!'" She seemed almost proud as she told the story of cornering the teacher and pressuring her into ridding the classroom of the child's presence. I immediately empathized with the teacher, picturing the irate mother asking the frustrated teacher to execute something she had no power to do.

"The teacher told me that she'd understand if I wanted to move my little 'Billy' to another class," Sharon said. My eyelid began to twitch. I imagined the poor teacher trying to appease this lady, who, judging by the emphatic way she was recounting the conversation, was not exactly polite.

"I told her that my little Billy is not moving, *that child is.*"

I cringed. The two other ladies at the table fell silent; they both knew that my son has an autism spectrum disorder and could very well cause similar disruptions. I, too, was speechless. This gathering consisted, after all, of Christian mothers. Where was the Christlike attitude?

So many thoughts race through my head at a moment like this. I decided to let this lady dig her own hole, which she seemed more than happy to do, telling stories of "that kid" dropping his pants in the classroom, among other things. I instantly recalled Alec's kindergarten teacher, Mrs. Belcher, telling me that my own son had come out of the bathroom recently, pants down, calling loudly for assistance.

For months, I'd been apprehensive about sending Alec to public school. Matt and I didn't have the money to pay the tuition for the local private school with a specialized program for autism, so we reluctantly placed him into our neighborhood school. Alec was a kindergarten student in his first month there. He was an inclusion student, which meant that he was a child with a developmental disability included in a classroom of neurotypical children. I agonized all of the previous summer, my mind imagining merciless conversations from other parents who'd be irritated that my son was creating a less-than-optimum learning environment for their children.

And here I was, actually listening to the words much like those I feared would be spoken to me regarding my own Alec. Sharon had reached into my heart and, without knowing, found my deepest nightmare. Her words had wrenched it out and tossed it casually on top of all of the smiling photographs of her children for all the other moms to see.

I tentatively asked Sharon a few questions. "Sharon, what grade is your son in?"

"Kindergarten," she answered, pasting a photo of her boy to a colored sheet of paper. By the way she was going on about it, you'd have thought it was a collegiate course instead of kindergarten.

Oh, kindergarten, of course, I thought. *Just like my Alec.* Parents, be aware that our enemy, Satan, knows exactly how to push our buttons. It was no coincidence that I was there at that moment, listening to words like those I'd imagined for months.

I asked if this child she was referring to could speak. "Oh, he speaks, but it's just a lot of nonsense."

Again, just like my Alec! Satan pushed a few more of my buttons, trying to find one that would launch a torpedo of insults with Sharon as the target.

So here was my dilemma: What should I do in this situation? A huge part of me wanted to dump my biggie-sized Diet Coke on her head. I actually spent a few moments thinking about this scenario. It was very tempting! Another part of me wanted to bring Alec along on our next scheduled scrapbook get-together so he could personally assist Sharon as she crafted her scrapbooks. I imagined him taking big handfuls of her photographs and chewing on them. Again, tempting . . .

The angry side of me wanted to verbally blast her. I'd quite a few choice words, an arsenal of insults rolling around in my head bursting to get out. But, really, what good would that do to either of us?

Educate, Don't Alienate: Speaking Out to Adults in the Community

A situation like this is not uncommon to parents of children with autism spectrum disorders. The offender could be a cynical teacher, an argumentative parent of a neurotypical child, a prickly neighbor, an uninformed church member, or even the woman giving you the stink eye in Target. These exchanges are typically unexpected, and although they are not always malicious—often they merely result from ignorance—they always produce a measure of hurt. They place us at ground zero in a sudden storm of raw emotion.

Rather than wait for the storm and act on reflex, we need to prepare for these encounters and have a plan for how we'll react. When the storm hits, it's up to us to know what to do. When we encounter another adult who is discussing our child, or any child with autism, in a manner we do not appreciate, we have three primary options: 1) launch a vocal counterattack; 2) choose to stay silent and ignore the comments; 3) choose to attempt to educate the person on the subject of autism. The tricky part is staying calm enough to decide how to respond!

Before you do anything . . . stop!

Take a breath, and call for some backup. This is a time to call in the cavalry and ask God for help. It doesn't have to be an elaborate prayer. Just take a moment and silently ask God for wisdom and ability to stand up against the assault.

As Sharon continued her tirade about the child in her son's classroom, I ushered up a call for some divine assistance: *Help me, Jesus! Help me know what to do!* I felt a trickle of sweat on my forehead, and my tongue felt dry and thick, like it was pasted with Elmer's glue to the roof of my mouth. *Help me do the right thing, God!*

We love our children and will do anything to defend them, so it's easy to choose option 1 and launch a verbal assault. I admit with regret that I've chosen this option in the past. When we choose this option in a vulnerable state of mind, however, it's easy to say something overly harsh that we'll later regret. In addition, if we choose this option we've missed out on a unique opportunity to turn the situation around to our advantage with God's help.

At certain times option 2—ignore the comments—is the correct choice. This would be primarily when you are extremely tired, ill, or agitated and you just need to step away from the situation because you know if you don't you're going to lash out in a ruthless way. When you need to choose this option, I hope that, after taking some time to gather your peace around you, you consider continuing to option 3 at a later time.

It's best to choose option 3—asking God to help us patiently educate the offender. When we do this, we outsmart our adversary, Satan, who would love for this situation to alienate us, and our children, from others. Satan wants us to counterattack, positioning ourselves against other parents and community members. So instead of lashing out as if this person is our enemy, we should make the most of this opportunity to establish an ally, something that would be far better for our children.

In my encounter with Sharon, after praying, I chose option 3 to help her walk a little in "that kid's" shoes. It was my hope that she become more sympathetic to children dealing with autism. I mustered up my nerve and gave her a crash course.

"Sharon," I said with some hesitation, "it sounds like this child might be autistic." Slowly and carefully and with God's direction, I chose my words. I did what I could to explain to Sharon what few options were available in kindergarten for this little boy. I described our school system's practice of inclusion, explaining what it means for both the disabled child and the neurotypical child. I also told her about the symptoms of autism and how prevalent it is today. I informed her that, with 1 in 150 children now diagnosed with an autism spectrum disorder, it wouldn't be surprising if this disruptive child was, indeed, autistic. I told her about Alec, and let her know that he had a lot to give others, even if his behavior was bizarre at times. Instead of spewing my frustrations at this parent, I relied solely on God's grace to give me the words to educate her.

Choosing option 3 can help someone better understand children on the autism spectrum. I believe God placed that mother at my table for a reason. It was one of my first steps in speaking out for the speechless.

Through my conversation with Sharon, Alec, who in many ways was similar to "that kid," became a real living and breathing boy to her. My prayer was that her heart would be open to compassion and acceptance of the boy in her son's classroom. Of course, only God can change a heart, and it has to be willing for change.

Although the emotion of that conversation blindsided me, God gave me the grace—and the words—to educate Sharon about children with autism and what they endure on a daily basis. It left the door open to acceptance: Sharon's acceptance of kids who are different from her son, and my own acceptance of parents who didn't want their child around a child like my son.

Yes, it's important for parents of children with autism to try to understand the concerns and fears of people like Sharon. I've often thought about her anger, trying to place myself in her shoes. Would I be as obsessed in making sure my neurotypical child's classroom provided the optimal environment for learning? Possibly I would. But we need to show others that children, even their children, can learn in many ways. Befriending a child with autism can be a wonderful experience for another child. Parents need to know that they don't have to fear our children. The way to do that is by sharing our story with them, and that takes guts.

Our children, though, are worth it, and I believe God will help us. Of course, not everyone will listen to us and accept our child, but you may be surprised at how many will. It's up to us to build that bridge, and God wants to help show us how. I wouldn't characterize Sharon's response to me as "converted," but she did appear surprised and to be pondering the information I'd given to her. At least I planted some seeds of thought.

I hope and pray that Alec, and all kids like him, are blessed with kids around them who are not afraid to embrace them despite their differences and, if needed, to speak out for them. When parents teach their kids to love others who are different, God always sends a kickback. I have a deep faith that each child who befriends Alec and others like him will get an incredible blessing in return.

Children can learn valuable life lessons from interacting with kids who have disabilities. Those kinds of lessons can't be taught in a book, but maybe they're the best lessons of all.

Speaking Out to Other ASD Parents: Words of Encouragement

It will happen one day.

Someone will walk up to you in a place you least expect—perhaps in the grocery store or at school or church—and will ask you for advice about autism. A father will tell you about some problems he's having with his son. A mother with a newly diagnosed child will come to you for help, wanting to know, "How can you smile when I feel like crying every waking minute?" You'll see in the eyes of that parent the same hollow look that you used to see in the mirror during your darker days of dealing with autism. They'll want to know how you've learned to accept autism, how you've managed to live with it, and, most of all, how you and your child have overcome it.

Are you ready to help? Are you willing to share in one of God's greatest miracles, as He uses the pain and hurt in your past to provide some light for someone else's walk? Oh, I know you're tired. And I know you may not want to drag out the old memories of the terrifying days when you were the parent dropped onto that dark road without a map. I know it can be difficult and intimidating to retrace your autism journey with a stranger, and that you'd probably much rather just hide behind the words, "Been there, done that."

I encourage you, however, to share your story with others—and not just because it will help *them*. One of my favorite promises of God is that He nourishes those who offer help to His children: "The one who gives a drink of water will receive water" (Prov. 11:25). I want you to reach out to others because in doing so, you actually help yourself and take a necessary step toward reclaiming the joy lost to the disorder.

God leaves fingerprints on our lives for all to see. Those prints tell the world that God exists and that His Word is true. We can find His fingerprints around us every day when we look for them. When you walk with God for a while, you'll begin to recognize His touch on the lives of others, too. When you reach out to touch the lives of others in need, rest assured, God reaches out to touch your life as well.

This is particularly evident when we reach out to others in need of support, including other parents on the autism journey. When we do so, God marks this kind of living with a spring of joy that bubbles over and never ends. Our journey here on earth becomes full of exciting experiences. A life lived in this way is an adventure as God brings people into our path, both to be blessed and to bring us blessing. Fingerprints of God become recognizable in the lives of those who choose to walk with Him and apply the promises of Scripture to life.

Helping Others Means Jumping into the Ditch with Them

My father may be short of stature, but he's full of wisdom that he has gained the hard way—from life knocking him down, kicking out his teeth, and leaving him to get back up ready for another round. One of the wisest things he taught me is that people who are hurting don't want someone to preach down at them from an elevated position of comfort. That approach requires so little effort on our part.

God wants more from His people. God wants His children to live lives that *matter*. If we are to leave a legacy of hope and make a difference in this world and in the lives of those around us, we need to help by grabbing a shovel, jumping into the ditch, and getting a little dirty.

People who are hurting are desperate for someone who will do more than simply offer advice. Our advice may be beneficial, but if that's all we give then it's similar to applying a Band-Aid to a broken arm—it doesn't do anything for the deeper issue (see James 2:15–16). People really crave authenticity, the kind they see when someone reaches out to lighten their load and to share their pain. These are qualities best exemplified in Christ Jesus. When God sees such qualities in a man, He promises to take care of that man (see Prov. 11:25 on the previous page).

Spurgeon calls this promise "divine recompense":

> If I carefully consider others, God will consider me, and in some way or other He will recompense me. Let me consider the poor, and the Lord will consider me. Let me look after little children, and the Lord will treat me as His child. Let me feed His flock, and He will feed me. Let me water His garden, and He will make a watered garden of my soul. This is the

Lord's own promise; be it mine to fulfill the condition and then to expect its fulfillment.[1]

I can hear you saying, "Yeah, right! How can I help other parents of children with autism when I have so many demands of my own? I can't even find time to breathe, let alone lighten anyone else's load!" Believe me, I understand how you feel. There are days when I can't check even one small task off of my weekly list. God knows this. He's not asking you to run for political office (although our communities need representatives who care about autism!) or to start a nonprofit to provide support for autism (although I know mothers who've done this quite successfully even while caring for their child). What God wants from us is a willing heart, and He knows it when He sees it. When He has that, He begins to work some magic into our very busy lives.

Reaching out is easier than you might think. God will place people around you daily, wherever you are—be it on the job, in the carpool line, in the park or doctor's office, even in your neighborhood—who can use a little encouragement and insight from your story. You can welcome ASD families into your own home socially, or even for home Bible studies, providing a place where their kids are welcome.

You can start by asking God to introduce you to other parents who could use a little encouragement and then start looking for them. I promise you that He will bring certain people into your life, parents who are anxious to see an example of Christ's love alive in your actions toward them and evidenced richly in your life. And let me tell you, that's when your walk with Christ gets exciting!

Speaking Out to Churches: It's Time to Ask for Help

It's Sunday, and Matt and I are in church, tired from another week of battling autism. At three years old, Alec has just been diagnosed with autism, and we're overwhelmed with the enormous prospect of caring for him. We've just finished the worship set, and Matt and I sink to our seats to drink in the sermon. As it begins, Matt jumps to the familiar buzz in his pocket, the pager summoning us to the children's wing. We hustle there and find Alec screaming hysterically, pushing himself on his back along the hallway. A confused volunteer explains that Alec began crying and, as she tried to hold him, his tantrum exploded.

We grew accustomed to calls to the nursery on a weekly basis, taking us away from the sermon that our thirsty souls needed. Alec had sensory issues, so holding him—especially during a meltdown—was terrifying to him. Sitting him down in a quiet corner would have helped, but Alec didn't have the verbal ability to express his needs. It's difficult for someone not familiar with autism's symptoms—which often include a hypersensitivity to noise, touch, or light—to know how to handle a child in the midst of a meltdown. It's difficult, but not impossible.

As a mother of an autistic child, I dreaded taking my son to Sunday school. I hoped it would go well, but knew there was a 95 percent chance that, before long, the pager would summon us back to retrieve our son. You might be thinking that it's easier not to go to church at all, and many parents do choose to stay home. Yet we parents of autistic children need the support and understanding that a church community can and should provide. After all, we're in the fight of our lives!

Many churches can and would help, but don't know how. So it's time to speak out to the churches, starting with our own, to let them know how they can minister to our unique families. Church leaders need to be aware of the increasing rate of autism and of ways to minister to these families in need. As parents of ASD kids we can do our part by vocalizing our needs. We can ask, for example, that our church provide at least one staff member or volunteer each Sunday who is trained to assist children with autism. We can tell them that the local Autism Society of America chapters can provide information about training volunteers to work with children on the autism spectrum. Explain that it's important for you to be able to attend a sermon so that you can be reenergized for the week ahead. Ask to meet with your child's Sunday school teachers to help them understand your child. During that meeting, you can also request that they teach lessons about the damaging effects of bullying. Don't just *ask* for things; offer help, too. Offer to help the church develop mentor programs and buddy systems for children with autism.[2]

Whenever Jesus wanted to illustrate the might of God's power and love, He did it by reaching out to the poor, the misunderstood, and the disabled. His was a compassionate ear to listen, and a touch that restored. Even shouldering the weight of the world, He took the time to address the children around Him (Luke 18:16). In doing so, His actions spoke in profound ways. A church founded in Scripture should want to do as Jesus did. If your church isn't willing to listen or help, then find a church that will! There are some wonderful churches out there that want to help. Don't settle for one that won't.

Speaking Out Politically: Defending Children with Autism

I never imagined that I, the introvert extraordinaire, would one day pick up a phone to call a state representative to ask for her support of autism-related issues. Nor did I envision marching to the nation's Capitol with 8,500 other parents to demand greener vaccines and individual inoculation schedules.[3] But that's exactly what I've done! I've found I can't be silent when I know that children with autism need a voice to speak for them in political matters. If we don't speak out, who will?

We will eventually discover the cause of the autism epidemic. Truth has a way of making itself known in time. It's like a seed buried under the snow; it seeks the light, desiring to be known and beheld by the world. One day the debate will end and we'll know why the frequency of autism cases began to skyrocket in the early 1990s, escalating from 1 in 10,000 to 1 in 150 as of the writing of this book.

In the meantime, let's continue to pray for the truth to be revealed, for an answer to the question of what is causing this autism epidemic. Parents must speak out, asking for answers to this question. Our representatives need to hear from us, and it's so easy to speak out. Simply pick up the phone or send an e-mail to your representatives and ask for funding for research projects that will provide proven treatments for autism.[4] Insist they vote for legislation beneficial to our cause and that will include governmental support for families dealing with autism. Your local Autism Society of America chapter can also let you know about legislative activity related to autism. We need to keep asking for help and keep knocking on doors. If we are to help our children, we must refuse to be silent.

Autism organizations do not need to agree on every issue in order to work together to solve the autism dilemma. When we unite to champion our children we are a formidable force. Remember this: our foe knows that a divided house will not stand. We can outsmart our adversary by refusing to allow our differences to divide us, which would minimize our combined strength. Let's work together to find the cause and seek the truth, but never forget that we are climbing the same mountain—autism!

That said, it's hard to write a book on autism without including a statement on the great debate: the issue of a relationship between childhood vaccines and autism. (No groaning, please!) This issue is divisive to say the least. Proponents of both sides are justifiably emotional, but if we are not careful to respect those with differing opinions, we will diminish the results of our efforts.

The issue of vaccine safety should be given consideration. Certainly everyone can agree that every measure needs to be taken to make childhood vaccines as safe as possible. We're placing our greatest gifts—our children—in the full trust of others to protect them. It should not be a blind trust. Parents must be able to trust the health care system, and if we are to do so, the dialogue must be forthright and honest. Let's agree on this much: we must push hard for answers until the cause of autism is determined beyond a shadow of a doubt.

Our children are depending on us!

God Will Give Us Words to Speak

God will help you speak out for your child. You and I may be only a couple of voices, but let's not forget that a powerful God stands with us. Remember God's promise to Moses when God called him to go before the most daunting of rulers, Egypt's Pharaoh, and demand the release of His people: "Now therefore go, I will be with your mouth and will teach you what you shall say" (Exod. 4:12). God was not asking Moses to "go it alone." God Himself was leading the way!

All parents of children with autism deserve the right to be heard. Choose to speak out for children with autism. When you do, remember that you are never alone. Remember that, even if you are shy and not eloquent, God promises to fill your mouth with His own words to defend and protect His precious ones. All you have to do is be willing to speak!

PROMISES TO TREASURE

Power to speak

But you will receive power when the Holy Spirit has come upon you, and you will be My witnesses in Jerusalem, in all Judea and Samaria, and to the ends of the earth.

—ACTS 1:8

Justice

These are the things you are to do: Speak the truth to each other, and render true and sound judgment in your courts.

—ZECHARIAH 8:16 (NIV)

Unity

May the God who gives endurance and encouragement give you a spirit of unity among yourselves as you follow Christ Jesus, so that with one heart and mouth you may glorify the God and Father of our Lord Jesus Christ.

—ROMANS 15:5–6 (NIV)

Truth

I have no greater joy than this: to hear that my children are walking in the truth.

—3 JOHN 1:4

Where Are We Now?

Living in the Promises of God

*I waited patiently for the LORD, and He turned to me and
heard my cry for help. He brought me up from a desolate
pit, out of the muddy clay, and set my feet on a rock, making
my steps secure. He put a new song in my mouth, a hymn of
praise to our God. Many will see and fear, and put their trust
in the LORD.*

PSALM 40:1–3

Alec is gone.

I turn around and look for my son, but he's not there. I scan the pool
from left to right, looking for a pair of bright green goggles. I search the
shallow end of our neighborhood pool where he was swimming only
moments before. Children are splashing and laughing. A boy jumps in
from the side of the pool and I think, *Oh, there he is!* But when the boy
surfaces, I see that I'm mistaken. It's not my son.

The sun is bright today, sparkling and dancing on the water. I put
my hand to my forehead to shield my eyes from the reflection as I approach the pool to get a closer look. No Alec.

Where can he be? Where is my son?

I turn and look past the fence into the playground, where Alec had
mentioned that he wanted to play. Several boys are tossing a yellow
ball. A child is sliding down the blue play set, but again, these children
are not mine. I look to the swings and find them empty, swaying only
slightly, evidence of the children who were there moments ago.

I turn back to the pool. "Alec?" I call over the sound of the laughter. There are more than twenty children romping in the three-foot deep area of the pool, but none of them answer to my call. A wave of fear rises within me. *Where's my son?*

As I wipe a hand across my brow, not sure if I'm sweating from the heat or from my anxiety, I recall a dream I had only a few nights before.

In the dream, I'm watching Alec from a distance as he hikes along a string of jagged boulders in a small river. The day is spilling with sunshine sparkling across the water as Alec carefully places each foot on the rocks, reaching down from time to time to steady himself. A woman is standing on the shore watching him. I hear no sound of the rushing water, but see only the vision of my boy mastering the rocks, water flowing around his tanned feet with each step.

Suddenly, as I watch, Alec slips. I see a mute splash, droplets of water flying high as if in slow motion, catching the sun in tiny prisms of light as they fall to join with the water below. As I stand there help-less, my son slips below the surface of the water, and he's gone from my sight.

My Alec is gone. Distraught with fear, I yell out to the woman standing by the water.

"Help him!" I scream, and she bends to the surface of the water and peers into it. I see confusion on her face. The woman searches, looks up to me and points to the water, but does not move.

"Get my son! Get him!" I cry as I begin to run, but my strides seem slow, delayed. I don't understand why she won't jump in to rescue him. *Why won't she move?* I run harder, but it feels like I'm running through waist-deep water. I'm making progress, but the river is still so far away. I need to get to my son! *Alec is only learning to swim,* I panic. *He can't save himself! I have to reach that river and get him out of the water!*

At long last I reach the river and stop at the edge, frantically search-ing the crystal water to see any sign of my son. I see nothing. Nothing at all.

I have to get him back! I have to bring him back to me! In the color-less water, I see large stones and forest debris along the river's bottom. Time is running out. I have to go now! The woman on the shore has a frustrated look on her face. I can see that she wants to help me, but doesn't know how. Looking down again, I see no sign of my son, but I can't delay another moment. The time is now to rescue my boy!

I jump headfirst into the river. I feel its coldness surround me as I dive. My hands reach the bottom and I run my fingers along the large rocks, brushing away the leaves and branches. I see nothing. I'm frantic.

Where is he? Where's my son?

I dig my arms deep into the debris. Dirt mixes with the water and now I can't see. Then, suddenly, my heart leaps. I touch something soft and familiar. It is smooth and warm, and I wrap my fingers around it and pull hard. It gives slightly, but not enough. I pull harder, using every ounce of energy I have. The murk rises in a brown cloud as I struggle to release Alec from the debris, but I don't seem to be strong enough. I clench both fists around the small hand and give my best pull, but the branches seem to tighten around him as I tug.

Can I do this? Can I get him?

Then something happens. Suddenly, I feel a strength that is not my own. My arms surge with new power, and I instinctively know that God is with me. I am not alone.

Another vigorous tug and a shape emerges from the rising murk. *It's my son. My Alec!* I pull again and encircle my arms around him, my beloved boy! Quickly, I swim with him to the surface, no longer aware of the coldness of the water. I lift my son up, up, past the surface and onto the muddy shore.

I clamber up, knees crunching on gravel, and kneel beside my boy. Streams of water run from my body to the ground, disappearing into the earth. I grab my son's shoulders and turn him over to study his chest, his face. *He's not breathing!* I take a long, deep breath and place my mouth on his mouth, pinching his nose shut. I exhale and feel his little chest expand. I sit up and watch him. Nothing.

Again, I take a breath and blow, feeling the rise in his chest.

Then, something miraculous happens. Alec coughs! He sputters and heaves, and water flows from his mouth and nose. With each blessed cough, the fluid is a heavenly sight, running down over his cheeks like rivers, little rivers of a life restored.

I want to share my joy with the woman, but when I look up, she's gone. She never knew my boy, nor did she possess the powerful love I had for him. That's why she couldn't help him—it could only be me. God worked through the intensity of the love I had for Alec, divine love that made me willing to give up everything to rescue another. Only through a conduit of sacrificial love, the kind of love a parent has for a child, did God provide the strength to rescue my son.

And suddenly, I know: my son is going to be okay. In this dream, I hear the beautiful music of my soul singing out to God in heaven, thanking Him for saving Alec. My boy is going to be just fine, and so am I.

The memory of the dream fades away. I'm standing on the edge of the shallow end of our neighborhood pool, but I still can't find Alec. A cruel vision comes to me, one of Alec at the bottom of this body of water. I search where the children are splashing, checking for something I never want to see. But I see no shapes—nothing out of the ordinary.

I look to the lifeguard chair at the shallow end of the pool, hoping that the young man seated there is keeping track of the chaos around him. He looks bored. I glance down to the other lifeguard, seated at the deep end of the pool. I study her as she watches a line of children jumping off of the diving board. Then something catches my eye.

Wait. Who is that? It can't be!

But it is. From across the pool I see a pair of bright green goggles. A brown-haired, pint-sized boy stands on the edge of the diving board. He bounces once, twice, and jumps with a splash into the deep end of the pool.

The deep end! My heart jumps. *He can't do that!*

I break out into a run, heading for the deep end, pushing aside small children and knocking over pool bags on the way. It seems as if I'm running in slow motion.

"Alec!" I yell. "Alec, what are you doing?" I'm certain I'll watch my son sink to the bottom of the pool.

Yet as I reach the deep water, I hear a voice from over my head.

"Hold on, Mom." It's the woman seated in the lifeguard chair. "I'm watching him. He's doing fine!"

I look back to the pool and see Alec swimming stroke by stroke, a little clumsy but buoyant, working his way to the ladder on the side of the twelve-foot end of the pool. "He can't do that," I explain, even as my son rises from the ladder, rivers of water streaming from his body, like rivers of life streaming down.

"He's fine, Mom." She's calm and seems surprised at my anxiety. "He's just hanging out with the other kids. I've been watching him. He's just fine."

"Look, Mama!" Alec calls to me, with a wet grin stretching from ear to ear. "Watch me!"

"Okay," I answer nervously.

My jaw hangs open as I watch Alec climb the steps to the diving board once again. He walks to the edge and jumps, making a big splash. My boy surfaces and looks around, then swims to the ladder. As the green goggles break the surface, he says to me, "Did you see that, Mom? Did you?" The sun is dancing across the droplets of water on his beautiful face. He is radiant; my boy is radiant with the light of God's love.

And as I stand there, that's what I see. I see God's love. I see God's faithfulness. And I see promises fulfilled.

Promises and Scars: Alec Today

Four years ago, I wept with two sweet ladies in the prayer room of my church. They held my hands and whispered words of love and encouragement to me, a frightened mother backed into a wall by a giant of a disorder. It threatened to steal Alec away from our family forever. One of those kind ladies looked into my eyes and whispered a promise that my son would be healed in God's sweet time. It was an impossible promise, but I took those words and wrapped them up, tucking them deeply into my heart.

I'm often asked, "Has Alec been healed?"

I've discovered that there are, in fact, very special blessings that come from raising a child with a special need. The veil has been lifted from my eyes, and I now see beauty where I used to see emptiness. There is compassion in me where there once was selfishness. There is laughter and fun where there used to be a constant mental rundown of tasks yet to be completed. There is even personal acceptance instead of feelings of inadequacy. I would not trade these gifts for the world.

Beyond a shadow of a doubt, I know this: *I* have been healed. Healed from selfishness. Healed from blindness to the suffering of others. I am no longer the same, and every change has been for the better.

But the question remains: Has Alec been healed?

I think about this question now that we've returned from our big day at the pool. I wonder, when God heals a person does His touch heal so completely that no evidence can be found of the former condition, or does He allow a scar to remain? I think the answer can be found in John's account of the resurrected Jesus appearing to His disciples:

> But one of the Twelve, Thomas (called "Twin"), was not with them when Jesus came. So the other disciples kept telling him, "We have seen the Lord!"
>
> But he said to them, "If I don't see the mark of the nails in His hands, put my finger into the mark of the nails, and put my hand into His side, I will never believe!"
>
> After eight days His disciples were indoors again, and Thomas was with them. Even though the doors were locked, Jesus came and stood among them. He said, "Peace to you!"
>
> Then He said to Thomas, "Put your finger here and observe My hands. Reach out your hand and put it into My side. Don't be an unbeliever, but a believer."
>
> Thomas responded to Him, "My Lord and my God!" (John 20:24–28)

Jesus had risen up in glorious victory over sin and death—yet He retained the scars of the crucifixion. He asked a doubting Thomas to reach out and touch those scars, and when Thomas did he believed the truth of the resurrection. Jesus' scars proved that God is far greater than any obstacle—even greater than death itself!

God is greater than autism, too.

In March of 2008, Matt, Alec, and I drove to Lynchburg, Virginia, to the Rimland Center to meet with Alec's doctor, Dr. Elizabeth Mumper. Impressed with Alec's progress, Dr. Mumper told us that Alec no longer required frequent visits. She placed him on a maintenance schedule of vitamin supplements. Although Alec remains on the gluten-free, casein-free, soy-free diet, Dr. Mumper has halted some of the interventions that we'd been utilizing for years. Alec no longer needs them.

Yes, God has delivered my son from the grip of autism and has enabled him to soar high above it. He speaks in clear sentences, when before he uttered only gibberish. His smile brightens any room he enters. Gone is the look of confusion and frustration that once dominated his countenance. He's quite a practical joker, laughing all of the time and pulling what he calls "tricks" on the family. He's a voracious reader, devouring any *Garfield* comic or *Captain Underpants* book he can get his hands on. Just this spring, he learned to ride a bike—no training wheels required—in a matter of ten minutes.

As I write this epilogue, Alec is on his way to second grade, and it's a typical classroom. Academically, he's on par with his classmates, and in some areas he's working beyond his grade level. The only area in which he is slightly behind is expressive writing. But even there he's improving.

Alec has been teased a little, but he makes friends easily. I'm forever humbled by the love that Alec's young classmates have shown in past years. Young Jarrod, for instance, ran extra laps so Alec wouldn't have to finish his run alone, and other children scribbled Crayola letters of encouragement that hang on our refrigerator, like this one from Cassie: "Wen we have a play deat you can play on the computr I do not care love Cassie." These children remind me that God is, indeed, very, very good.

Miraculous progress aside, there are still faint scars of autism in Alec's life. They fade with the years, but I expect we will always be able to detect them. Do the scars mean my prayer warrior was wrong? Should I hope for a healing with no trace of autism?

It seems to me that just as Jesus retained the scars of the crucifixion, there are scars that remain with us. These scars speak of the battles that God has carried us through, forever reminding us that we have been rescued. They remind us that ours is a glorious Lord, a powerful Savior and Redeemer, and that He loves us more than we can comprehend. The scars are records of our testimonies, begging to be shared with others we meet, those who are in need and are searching for a lifeline in a sea of trouble. We pull up our sleeves and show them our scars, telling them our salvation story and sharing the promises of God, our Deliverer. In this we glorify God.

It's been four years since I sat with my sweet prayer warriors, and each time I look at my son I feel as if I'm beholding a miracle. He plays outside with the children on the street and rides his bike everywhere. He wrapped up his first season on the neighborhood swim team, winning the "Most Improved" award for the season. He argues with his big sister, Elise. (Yes, this is a blessing when you consider for years he did not speak!) He can now communicate in regular sentences. He has friends in the classroom, and, better still, he is a good friend to others as well.

Each time I see Alec's faint scars, I remember how far God has brought us. They tell the story of how God reached down to pull Alec from a dark, murky place, and restored him to the boy he was intended to be. It's the story of a God who revealed Himself to Alec, before he could form the words to say a single spoken prayer. And it's the story of a God who empowered me to be the mother Alec needed, even when I felt I couldn't go on another day.

I have decided that I would rather die with the hope of possessing every single one of God's promises than to live a life without hope. That's because I know that life is a journey, a process. The goal is always in sight, but it's the getting there that is glorious. I've decided that I will love today as it is. And I will continue to press on, striving for all that God has for me and for my son.

So, has my son been healed? Words from this afternoon at the pool come to mind. "Did you see me, Mom?" spoken by a boy who is no longer afraid. And I remember the words of the lifeguard, a stranger who looked at my son and did not see autism: "He's just hanging out with the other kids. I've been watching him. He's just fine." And I believe with all of my heart that my son, Alec, has been strengthened in his journey with autism. I believe that boy is going to change the world!

This Is God's Story

So many times I was blinded by our family circumstances. My eyes were locked on autism itself, a mountain that had captured the entire field of my vision. As I began our autism journey, I couldn't see past the mountain. I couldn't see that God was simply writing another chapter in the book of my life and the life of my son, a book not about autism at all. Instead, it's a book about God, a tale of the heavenly Father reaching out to pull us toward Home.

God has been the one kneeling before us when we have turned from Him, the same way that Alec turned inward on the day my eyes were opened to his isolation and need. We are the ones who, like little flowers, have turned from the sunshine, His light, as if unworthy of its love. It's God who bends down to us, tenderly grasping our chins and lifting our tear-stained faces to see past autism, to see only Him. When we look to Him, I promise you this—the darkness of autism is entirely overcome by His radiance.

Overcoming is, in fact, God's story, written across the centuries and penned by many authors. All of Scripture, its words breathed into existence by a living God, and all of the promises it contains, are a love letter from God meant for each of us. The promises are God's covenant, proof that we are His children. With those promises, He pulls us from the muck of this world and makes us to walk as royal children of the Most High God.

Dear friends, as we walk in the shadow of autism, God is whispering to us, "Hold on! I'm coming to get you!" Despite autism's grasp on your family, God reaches out to hold on to you—with every ounce of His being . . . for eternity. "I will help you," He whispers. "Nothing is impossible for Me!"

Believe it, and know that the promises of God are for you and your child, given by a God who sees every mountain standing in your way and urges you to look beyond to the mountaintop that He has prepared for you and your child.

Can you see it now? Run to it! It's just up ahead!

> The Lord has promised good to me,
> His word my hope secures;
> He will my shield and portion be
> As long as life endures.
>
> JOHN NEWTON, "AMAZING GRACE," 1779

Appendix A

What Is Autism?

Autism is a complex developmental disability that typically appears during the first three years of life. It affects a child's ability to communicate and interact with others. Autism is defined by a certain set of behaviors and is a "spectrum disorder" that affects individuals differently and to varying degrees. There is no known single cause for autism, but increased awareness and funding can help families today.

In February 2007, the Centers for Disease Control and Prevention issued their ADDME autism prevalence report. The report, which looked at a sample of eight-year-olds in 2000 and 2002, concluded that the prevalence of autism had risen to 1 in every 150 American children, and almost 1 in 94 boys.

Currently, the Autism Society of America estimates that the lifetime cost of caring for a child with autism ranges from $3.5 million to $5 million, and that the United States is facing almost $90 billion annually in costs for autism. This figure includes research, insurance costs and noncovered expenses, Medicaid waivers for autism, educational spending, housing, transportation, employment, in addition to related therapeutic services and caregiver costs.

Know the Signs: Early Identification Can Change Lives

Autism is treatable. Children do not "outgrow" autism, but studies show that early diagnosis and intervention lead to significantly improved outcomes.

Here are some signs to look for in the children in your life:

- Lack of or delay in spoken language
- Repetitive use of language and/or motor mannerisms (e.g., hand flapping, twirling objects)
- Little or no eye contact
- Lack of interest in peer relationships
- Lack of spontaneous or make-believe play
- Persistent fixation on parts of objects[1]

Autism Resources

Recommended Books

Hamilton, Lynn. *Facing Autism: Giving Parents Reasons for Hope and Guidance for Help.* Colorado Springs: WaterBrook Press, 2000. A mother's account of trying many "alternative" therapies for her son with autism, including Applied Behavior Analysis (ABA). Written from a Christian perspective, the book contains lists of resources (institutes, clinics, schools, and programs, with phone and FAX numbers, e-mail addresses, and Web sites).

Maurice, Catherine, Gina Green, and Stephen C. Luce. *Behavioral Intervention for Young Children with Autism: A Manual for Parents and Professionals.* Austin, TX: Pro-Ed, 1996. This book has been called the bible for home-based ABA programs. It is a thorough, educational, and detailed work that includes the science behind ABA, what and how to teach, organizing and funding, and more.

McCarthy, Jenny. *Louder Than Words: A Mother's Journey in Healing Autism.* New York: Plume, 2008. This book is a telling of McCarthy's experience with her son Evan's autism. It is an autobiographical account and includes a good amount of humor. It reinforces the need for parents to forcefully engage the health care system. Be prepared for profanity.

Recommended Web Sites

Autism Organizations

Autism Society of America (www.autism-society.org) offers a wealth of information including a directory of local chapters, current research, an e-newsletter, programs and support, daily tips, and even a list of sensory friendly films.

Autism Speaks (www.autismspeaks.org) is particularly helpful in disseminating information about legislation that relates to autism and how to become involved on a local level.

Autism Research Institute (www.autism.com) conveys information about the science behind the causes of and treatments for autism. It informs about the triggers of autism as well as methods of diagnosis and treating autism. The site is aimed at individuals, families, and health care providers, and lists how parents rate various treatments.

Coalition for SafeMinds (www.safeminds.org) is a private nonprofit organization founded to investigate and raise awareness of the risks to infants and children of exposure to mercury from medical products, including thimerosal in vaccines. SafeMinds supports research on the potential harmful effects of mercury and thimerosal.

Defeat Autism Now! (www.defeatautismnow.com) is dedicated to the exploration, evaluation, and dissemination of scientifically documented biomedical interventions for individuals within the autism spectrum, through the collaborative efforts of clinicians, researchers, and parents. This site provides a list of clinicians using the Defeat Autism Now! approach, alerts for Defeat Autism Now! conferences, and addresses the physiological disorders and medical conditions that lie at the core of autistic disorders.

Families for Early Autism Treatment (www.feat.org) is a nonprofit organization of parents, family members, and treatment professionals dedicated to providing information about education, advocacy, and support. The FEAT Web site discusses FEAT's goals and organization, and how FEAT can help families and individuals directly. It also provides information about other helpful resources. Not available in every state.

First Signs (www.firstsigns.org) is dedicated to the early identification of and intervention for children with autism and other related disorders. The site offers information about screening, diagnosis, and treatment.

Generation Rescue (www.generationrescue.org) is an international movement of scientists, physicians, and parent-volunteers researching the causes and treatments for autism, and mentoring thousands of families in recovering their children from autism. Jenny McCarthy and Jim Carrey are board members.

National Autism Association (www.nationalautismassociation.org) offers free printable brochures. The site contains a wealth of information from greening schools to keeping marriages together. The site also offers links to conferences, fund-raisers, national news videos, nutrition information, more.

Talk About Curing Autism (www.talkaboutcuringautism.org) provides information, resources, and support to families affected by autism. For families who have just received the autism diagnosis, TACA aims to speed up the cycle time from the autism diagnosis to effective treatments. TACA helps to strengthen the autism community by connecting families and the professionals who can help them, allowing them to share stories and information to help people with autism be the best they can be.

Unlocking Autism (www.unlockingautism.org) offers links to a parent-to-parent network, articles about autism in the news, congressional testimonies, and more. The site also sponsors a blog.

Autism Related Books

Autism Society of North Carolina Bookstore (www.autismbookstore
.com) offers over six hundred titles related to autism, reader recommendations, software, DVDs, and general merchandise.

Christian Inspiration for Autism

Children of Destiny (www.childrenofdestiny.org) is the Web site of
Jack and Rebecca Sytsema, ordained ministers. They seek to bring
together traditional science and medicine with recently developed
and recognized treatments and therapies to establish the preemi-
nent center for treatment, education, and research for the cure of
autism and other developmental disabilities. The Sytsemas firmly
hold to the belief that the most powerful intervention they have
brought into the life of Nicholas, their son who has autism, has
been to give him over to God and allow Him to order their steps
concerning their son.

Government Resources

CDC's Autism Information Center (www.cdc.gov/ncbddd/autism/)
informs about CDC and congressional activity; resources for families, educators, and practitioners; publications and databases.

National Institute of Mental Health (www.nimh.nih.gov/health/
topics/autism-spectrum-disorders-pervasive-developmental
-disorders/index.shtml) offers science news, ASD publications,
NIH activities, and more.

U.S. Department of Health & Human Services (www.acf.hhs.gov/
programs/add/) provides original documentation on government programs and findings. Entering the keyword "autism" in
the search function for this site will result in numerous links to
autism-related topics on the site.

Information on Autism Legislation

Autism Votes (www.autismvotes.org) informs about what is currently happening in the legislature, insurance reform, and more, plus offers links to information about how to become politically involved.

Kelly Langston Web Sites

Author's blog (www.kellylangston.com), *Autism's Hidden Blessings* Web site with community support (www.autismshiddenblessings.com), and Walking with Alec blog (www.walkingwithalec.com).

News Resources

Age of Autism (www.ageofautism.com) is a "daily web newspaper of the autism epidemic," offering news and information on a wide range of topics related to autism including finances, vaccines, research, legal cases, nutritional supplements, and more.

Autism Hangout (www.autismhangout.com) reports news and compiles facts and community-submitted personal experiences to discern how best to deal with the daily challenges of autism.

Autism One Radio (www.autismone.org/radio/) is community livestream talk radio discussing ideas, change, and recovery.

Autism Society of America News (www.autism-society.org/site/Page Server?pagename=asa_news) is the news page of the ASA Web site featuring links to a wide range of information: conferences, politics, toys, teaching reading, scientific studies, even gluten-free recipes.

Support for Special Diets

The Autism Network for Dietary Interventions (www.autismndi.com) states that its purpose is to help parents understand, implement and maintain dietary intervention for their autistic children. The site offers a wide range of information on dietary interventions. Enter keyword "recipes" to access links to gluten-free recipes.

Appendix C

Straight Talk from a Dad

Note from Kelly: I've always admired the way my husband, Matt, takes a strong and active role in our family journey with autism. So I asked him if he had any advice especially for other fathers who, like him, are raising a child with autism. I'm thankful that he accepted the opportunity! The following are some very candid suggestions from Alec's daddy. They are listed in his own words, and written specifically to other fathers walking with autism.

As much as we may wish it, autism is not something that can be fixed with a screwdriver or a wrench—or duct tape for that matter. Even so, there are many things we dads can do:

1. Understand that our financial support does matter. The treatment of autism is expensive. The efforts we make through our jobs to help support our families and pay for treatments do provide benefit. It's important to remind ourselves that we're a part of the solution, and God is going to use us, as well as the moms.

2. Understand that we didn't "mess up" or cause this to happen, so we shouldn't blame ourselves.

3. Support our wives. Practically speaking, it is unlikely that the burden of an autistic child will be borne equally by both spouses. Don't forget to contribute to maintaining the mental health of your wife!

4. Your son or daughter is still there! Although your child with autism may have communication difficulties ranging from mild to severe, your child is still in there—merely behind the cloak of autism. These kids have personalities and great senses of humor, and there is joy for you to find by taking the time to seek out your child.

5. Get involved! Go to an autism conference or be a part of an autism group. You'll be better able to make choices for your child about treatments and therapies. Don't wait for your wife to do all of the research. It is immensely helpful for you to understand what's going on and what the various treatments are supposed to do. The more you can understand the treatment options, the better financial choices you'll be able to make.

6. Don't check out! It saddens me to see the numbers for divorce rates among families dealing with autism. Don't ignore your autistic child and his or her special needs. Your child needs you to be a dad and to participate in his or her treatments and therapies. Your neurotypical children, too, need you to be present and active in their lives. Your wife needs you to be a husband to her and a father to your children. It's hard work, but it's what a man does, and you'll have a great sense of satisfaction when you see your child with autism making progress. Bearing this burden alone is terribly difficult for a single parent.

7. Even if you're divorced, don't just disappear. Your former spouse may be your "ex" wife, but your children are never your "ex" children. For the sake of your autistic child, you need to communicate with your ex and keep a cohesive treatment regimen for your child. This suggestion applies to mothers as well. I've heard stories of custody situations where one parent followed a treatment program, only to have it undone by his or her ex the following week, on the custody/visitation schedule. Dietary restrictions are one example—if one parent is using a gluten-free/casein-free diet for the child, and the other parent during the following week is feeding the kid milkshakes and wheat pancakes, the diet will have no benefit at all. Everyone

loses. So make sure you're on the same page—for your child's sake!

8. Commit to keeping the family together, no matter what it takes. Your family is the legacy you will leave behind.

Notes

Preface

1. A number of similar symptoms are present in those diagnosed with autism, yet these symptoms can range from very mild in one person to very severe in another. Because of this, health care providers refer to autism as a "spectrum" disorder. If a child is autistic, he or she has what is medically termed as an "autism spectrum disorder."

Chapter 1: God's Promises

1. Charles Haddon Spurgeon, *Faith's Checkbook: A Devotional*, preface, Accordance Bible Software CD-ROM, version 1.0, OakTree Software, Inc.
2. Ibid.
3. Ibid.
4. Ibid.

Chapter 2: The Anchor of Our Lifeline

1. Warren W. Wiersbe, *The Wiersbe Bible Commentary: Old Testament* (Colorado Springs: David C. Cook, 2007), 29.
2. Spurgeon, *Faith's Checkbook*, December 14.
3. Ibid., July 28.

Chapter 3: The Blessings Behind the Giants

1. Defeat Autism Now! conferences "provide the latest information for parents and professionals, information that leads to medical treatment and metabolic support sufficient to reduce physical

pain and roadblocks in children with autism, to the extent that many are newly able to communicate and learn. Defeat Autism Now!® is distinguished by its commitment to invite only the most credible, accredited, and forward-thinking researchers and clinicians as speakers." Quote is courtesy of Jane Johnson, Director of Defeat Autism Now! See www.defeatautismnow.com for more information.

While not every child responds to the Defeat Autism Now! protocols, many families report that their children have been helped by them. Our son, Alec, was one who did respond in a dramatic way. We saw significant improvements in Alec's behavior and ability to communicate as directed by a clinician pursuing the Defeat Autism Now! approach. Alec is a patient of Dr. Elizabeth Mumper, MD, President and CEO of the Rimland Center located in Lynchburg, Virginia. Dr. Mumper is the Medical Director of the Autism Research Institute and a national speaker.

2. As an autism therapy, Applied Behavioral Analysis, or ABA, uses behavioral approaches to teach appropriate behavior and cognitive skills to children. A given task is broken into smaller steps with positive reinforcements offered for correct responses to each step. Data is recorded and analyzed to verify improvements.

"Mental Health: A Report of the Surgeon General," the collaborative report by the National Institutes of Health (NIH) and the Substance Abuse and Mental Health Services Administration (SAMHSA), states, "Thirty years of research demonstrated the efficacy of applied behavioral methods in reducing inappropriate behavior and in increasing communication, learning, and appropriate social behavior." See www.surgeongeneral.gov/library/mentalhealth/chapter3/sec6.html#autism, September 2009.

Chapter 4: The Dawn Will Surely Come

1. Wiersbe, *Wiersbe Bible Commentary: Old Testament*, 85.
2. John Wesley, "Notes on the Gospel of John, Chapter 4" in *Notes*

on the Whole Bible, Accordance Bible Software CD-ROM, version 1.1, OakTree Software, Inc.

3. James Strong, *Strong's Greek Dictionary of the New Testament,* s.v. "parakletos," Accordance Bible Software CD-ROM, version 2.3, OakTree Software, Inc.

Chapter 5: Revelations Without Words

1. Phil Vischer, "Thankfulness Song," © Bob and Larry Publishing, 2002. All rights reserved. Used with permission.

2. See chapter 3, note 1.

3. Verbal behavior is an approach used to teach language and communication skills. Based on the research of B. F. Skinner in verbal behavior programs, the specific wants and desires of a child are considered and then the child is taught how to make a request for that want by using a word, or sign language, or even reaching for the item. In a verbal behavior inclusion program, children with autism are integrated with neurotypical children in an educational setting, and educators employ the verbal behavioral programs within the included setting. A benefit of the inclusion setting is that it helps teach acceptance of children with special needs.

4. For more information about Vital Interventions Accessible, see www.vianow.org.

5. There is an ongoing controversy about the link between vaccines, the mercury-based preservative thimerosal, and autism. According to the Centers for Disease Control and Preventions (CDC), "Since 2001, with the exception of some influenze (flu) vaccines, thimerosal is not used as a preservative in routinely recommended childhood vaccines." The CDC states, "evidence from several studies examining trends in vaccine use and changes in autism frequency does not support such an association" (www.cdc.gov/vaccinesafety/concerns/thimerosal.htm).

Many parents of children with autism, including this author, call for safer vaccine programs to include safe vaccine ingredients, schedules, and dosages modified to the individual patient rather

than a one-size-fits-all program. See www.generationrescue.org/
vaccines.html for more information.

6. Jill Urwick, in a personal account given to author, November 14,
2005. Used with permission.

7. Ibid.

8. Helen Keller and Annie Sullivan, *The Story of My Life*, ed. John
Albert Macy (New York: Doubleday, Page, and Co., 1905), 203.

9. Helen Keller, *My Religion* (New York: Book Tree, 2007), 29.

10. Ibid., 31.

11. Keller Johnson-Thompson, "Ask Keller," Helen Keller Kids
Museum Online, www.afb.org/braillebug/askkeller.asp?issueid
=20073 (March 2007). Used by permission of Ms. Johnson-
Thompson, the American Foundation for the Blind, and the
Helen Keller Foundation.

12. Helen Keller, "Mine to Keep," as quoted in "Ask Keller," www
.afb.org/braillebug/askkeller .asp?issueid=20073.

Chapter 6: Making Sense of a Confusing Disorder

1. Matt and I have found that Alec has an enhanced ability to focus,
better eye contact, and improved communication skills while following a diet without gluten, casein, and soy. A number of medical studies have found that many ASD children have food aller-
gies resulting from an immune system dysfunction that affects
the body's ability to break down certain proteins and effectively
fight off yeasts and bacteria. A listing of these studies and explanations of the science behind them can be found at the Autism
Research Institute Web site, or specifically at www.autism.com/
treatable/index.htm.

2. Due to digestive problems, and in Alec's case refusal to eat a
balanced diet due to food sensory issues, some children with
autism show, after medical testing, a deficiency in a number
of essential nutrients. Supplementation can help replace these
nutrients and improve the overall physical health of children
with autism. Presentations that explain the science behind the

supplementation protocol can be found at www.autism.com/ danwebcast/supplements.htm.

Chapter 7: The Greatest Therapy

1. Wiersbe, *Wiersbe Bible Commentary: Old Testament*, 916.

Chapter 9: When the Bully Taunts

1. Deuteronomy 26:18; Isaiah 49:16; Galatians 3:29.
2. Spurgeon, *Faith's Checkbook*, May 4.

Chapter 10: What Eye Has Not Seen nor Ear Has Heard

Epigraph. Jim Carrey, speaking at the Green Our Vaccines rally in Washington, DC on June 4, 2008. See CNN video "Fighting Autism" at www.cnn.com/video/?/video/showbiz/2008/06/05/ riminton.carey.mccarthy.autism.cnn. Carrey is referring to Jenny McCarthy's son Evan, who was diagnosed with autism.

Chapter 11: Strength for the Weary Heart

1. Susan DeFord, "No Group Discount for Autism Care," *Washington Post*, June 3, 2007, www.washingtonpost.com/wp-dyn/ content/article/2007/06/02/AR2007060200627.html.

Chapter 12: From Speechless to Unspeakable Joy

1. Robert J. Dean, *The Holman Illustrated Bible Dictionary* (Nashville: Holman Bible Publishers, 2003), 956. Used by permission of Lifeway Christian Resources.
2. Wiersbe, *Wiersbe Bible Commentary: Old Testament*, 777.
3. IEP, Individualized Education Program. This educational program, mandated by the Individuals with Disabilities Education Act, requires schools to provide a unique program for every student who has a disability and who meets requirements. Typically, parents attend an IEP meeting to prepare the education program for their child.

Chapter 13: Speaking Out for the Speechless

1. Spurgeon, *Faith's Checkbook*, January 10.
2. Your local Autism Society of America chapter can help you find information about mentor and buddy programs. You can locate your local chapter at www.autism-society.org/site/PageServer?pagename=community_chapters.
3. For more detailed information about the call for greener vaccines, see Generation Rescue, www.generationrescue.org. Generation Rescue is an autism research and treatment advocacy organization. It is an international movement of scientists, physicians, and parent-volunteers researching the causes and treatments for autism, and mentoring thousands of families in recovering their children from autism. Jenny McCarthy—author, activist, and ASD mom—is a board member.
4. For contact information for your federal, state, and local officials, see www.congress.org/congressorg/home/.

Appendix A: What Is Autism?

1. "About Autism," *Autism Society of America*, www.autism-society.org/site/PageServer?pagename=about_home. Text used by permission of the American Autism Society of America.

About the Author

Kelly Langston is passionate about the extraordinary adventure of walking hand-in-hand with a God that loves us more than we can comprehend. She has written professionally since her early days in the journalism school of Ohio State University, where she wrote for the *Lantern*. Kelly's articles have appeared in *P31 Magazine* of Proverbs 31 Ministries and focus on her continual hunt to discover God's fingerprint in every gift that life brings.

Married to Matt and mother of two vivacious children, Kelly now runs a Charlotte-based company, Langston Marketing Services, specializing in Internet communications and Web development. Her blog Walking with Alec has resonated with parents of autistic children from around the world. Kelly has marched in Washington for autism issues and is blessed with the friendship of parents who live to make a difference for children with autism.

To contact Kelly, visit www.autismshiddenblessings.com or www.kellylangston.com.